THE NETWORKED PUBLIC

Amber Sinha is a lawyer interested in technology, the Internet, and how the law engages with them. He is interested in the impact of emerging technologies on existing legal frameworks, and how they need to evolve in response. He works at the Centre for Internet and Society, where he manages programs on privacy, big data, digital identity and artificial intelligence. Amber has taught at the National Law School of India University, Bangalore and Christ University, Bangalore. Prior to a life in public policy, Amber worked as a corporate lawyer.

Praise for the book

As our honourable Supreme Court has rightly pointed out, Amber Sinha is an important emerging scholar at the intersection of the Internet and the society. His first book focuses on disinformation in India and provides students, researchers, policy makers and the general public with a comprehensive theoretical and empirical survey, while, at the same time, being a thoroughly enjoyable read.

—**Sunil Abraham**, Executive Director,
The Centre for Internet and Society, Bangalore

THE NETWORKED PUBLIC

How Social Media is Changing Democracy

AMBER SINHA

RUPA

Published by
Rupa Publications India Pvt. Ltd 2019
7/16, Ansari Road, Daryaganj
New Delhi 110002

Sales centres:
Allahabad Bengaluru Chennai
Hyderabad Jaipur Kathmandu
Kolkata Mumbai

Copyright © Amber Sinha, 2019

The views and opinions expressed in this book are the author's own and the facts are as reported by him/her which have been verified to the extent possible, and the publishers are not in any way liable for the same.

All rights reserved.
No part of this publication may be reproduced, transmitted, or stored in a retrieval system, in any form or by any means, electronic, mechanical, photocopying, recording or otherwise, without the prior permission of the publisher.

ISBN: 978-93-5333-672-1

First impression 2019

10 9 8 7 6 5 4 3 2 1

The moral right of the author has been asserted.

Printed by Nutech Print Services, Faridabad

This book is sold subject to the condition that it shall not, by way of trade or otherwise, be lent, resold, hired out, or otherwise circulated, without the publisher's prior consent, in any form of binding or cover other than that in which it is published.

To the trials and tribulations of the Indian democracy,
'the most reckless political experiment in human history'.

Contents

Introduction   1

PART ONE
Public Access to (Mis)Information

Chapter 1: Making Sense of Misinformation   19
Chapter 2: The New Gatekeepers   39

PART TWO
The Irrational Public

Chapter 3: WhatsApp's Misinformation Menace   57
Chapter 4: The Limitations of Fact-checking   71

PART THREE
In Search of the Public

Chapter 5: The Suspect Science of Political Targeting   89
Chapter 6: The Political Economy of Data   105
Chapter 7: The Unholy Networks of Power   117

PART FOUR
Failures of Public Institutions

Chapter 8: Systematic Compromise of Institutions   131
Chapter 9: The Election Commission's Crisis of Credibility   147

PART FIVE
Public Forums of Internet Platforms

Chapter 10: Regulating Internet Intermediaries   165
Chapter 11: Platforms as Public Spheres   177

Acknowledgements   203
Endnotes   205

Introduction

These various remedies, eugenic, educational, ethical, populist and socialist, all assume that either the voters are inherently competent to direct the course of affairs or that they are making progress towards such an ideal. I think [democracy] is a false ideal.

—Walter Lippmann, political commentator, The Phantom Public

Democracy in Crisis

As the world's largest democracy concluded its seventeenth general election in seventy-two years, there appeared to be a growing trend of democratic constitutional crisis across the world. Countries like South Africa, Venezuela, Hungary, Poland and Turkey are some prominent examples of the systematic erosion of constitutional democratic values. Alongside, there has also been a gradual but definite compromise of the democratic process in the United States (US), Spain, United Kingdom (UK) and Egypt. In a recent volume on democratic crisis across various countries,[1] several descriptive terms for what we are witnessing were put forth—'democracy in retreat', 'democratic deconsolidation',[2] 'democratic backsliding',[3] 'democratic recession',[4] 'constitutional retrogression',[5] 'constitutional failure'[6] and 'constitutional rot'.[7] While all of these terms mean separate things, this abundance of scholarly descriptions indicates a growing problem that has not only been witnessed in several countries in the last decade, but has also been given due recognition. One doesn't want to be an alarmist, and so it is important to note that this is hardly the first time that we are witnessing such a phenomenon. Rather, some would argue that this is part of a cyclical trend seen every few decades or so—even in the last century and a half. We don't have to look too far for an example—in India, the declaration of the Emergency by the Indira Gandhi-led government in 1975–77 led to the erosion of several public institutions. Some of them recovered in the face of public backlash.

Through the second half of the twentieth century, there was a marked increase in the number of democracies. In the first two decades, this had a lot to do with regimes gaining independence from European imperialism, and being available for conversion to liberal democratic governments. Over time, one also saw a clear increase in the adoption of constitutional democratic practices within these countries, and a mostly steady consolidation and strengthening of these practices. However, in the last decade or so, we have witnessed a reversal of this trend. This reversal is not necessarily in the form of an illegal ousting of democracies for dictatorships, but through a steady accumulation of power within the democratic constitutional setup (discussed in *Chapter 10*). This form of democratic backsliding involves authoritarian actors continuing to operate within the framework of constitutional legitimacy, but significantly compromising mechanisms of accountability.

Several common trends mark this phenomenon globally. Anti-immigrant sentiment, religious fundamentalism and increased tribalism all threaten a pluralistic, dynamic society, often considered vital for a democracy to thrive in.[8] With growing international immigration and refugee crises, right-wing nationalism based on racial, ethnic and religious identities has become the de facto response. More significantly, these movements have inevitably led to greater accumulation of power in the hands of a few, the undermining of institutions and the chipping away of mechanisms that hold those in power accountable. There is also impatience with democratic institutions and their need for consensus. Rather than seeing the value such consensus brings, they are increasingly viewed as impediments to rapid economic growth and development. Instead, there is much greater acceptance of the authoritative regimes, in the hope that they will bring about good governance and foster development.[9]

Misinformation and Extreme Speech

The developments described above have been accompanied, both in India and elsewhere, with a culture of growing misinformation, hate speech and abuse—especially online. That is not to say that such speech does not or has not existed on more traditional mediums like television and print. Today, we most commonly see problematic speech online—on social media, online messaging services, monetized pages on Internet platforms dependent on advertising revenue, and partisan blogs and websites. It is not at all difficult to come across both public figures and the general public using such speech. This book deals with the two primary versions of problematic speech: the first is 'misinformation', discussed in *Chapter 3*, which involves the creation and sharing of intentionally or unintentionally false information; and the second, dealt with in lesser detail, is the practice of hate speech, abusive language and online harassment, which we refer to as 'extreme speech'.

Misinformation and extreme speech are usually designed to achieve one or more of the following objectives:

To Raise Ideological Issues
They are used to raise issues that are directly related to the ideological shifts described above, such as religious polarization, anti-immigrant sentiment and the devaluing of democratic institutions as hindrances to economic growth. This can be done through a story that introduces a problem, often using its narrative technique to identify heroes and villains right away.

To Set an Agenda
In the run-up to the elections, viral posts in support of different parties are framed as binary messages deifying one figure and denigrating the other. Here, it plays an agenda-setting role.

To Misdirect
The next kind of use is to deflect and obfuscate, usually in an attempt to maintain or wrest back control of the narrative. It is often achieved by using logical fallacies, but also resorting, at times, to abuse. This phenomenon is easily explained with behaviour that has become popular in online discourse—'whataboutery', which is the act of not responding to a specific critique but raising tangentially related or unrelated issues to deflect attention.

To Ridicule
Finally, such speech is also used to ridicule and character-assassinate. Communication scholar and social anthropologist Sahana Udupa has described it as best captured in the Hindi word 'gaali', which simultaneously cuts across 'the blurred boundaries of comedy, insult, shame and abuse'.[10]

Misinformation and extreme speech are the key markers of a world where societies are moving away from critical thinking. Critical thinking requires an appreciation of historical contexts, unbiased engagement with opposing viewpoints and the examination of rational truths. For critical thinking to succeed as a public process, we need forums that not only encourage participation, but also facilitate meaningful analysis and dialogue. In the past, such critical thinking would take place in educational institutions, the mass media, and both private and public political discussions. Each of these forums was accompanied by its own checks and balances—educational institutions relied on mechanisms of quality control and academic rigour such as peer reviews; fact-checking tried to ensure the veracity of information in the media; and in private and public discussions, there were well-understood codes of conduct for civil engagement. These systems, while far from perfect, have had the advantage of time to evolve and improve. At the very least, we have had the chance to assess the limitations of these forums and consider solutions for them. The ubiquity, virality and accessibility of Internet platforms, and the potential for unfettered dissemination that they offer, is fundamentally different from pre-web forums. At the time of writing this book, there were over 600 million Internet users in India, with about 260 million people on Facebook, and over 200 million monthly active users on WhatsApp.[11] Despite the sheer volume of participation, it is still very much early days in the development of tools and guidelines for online spaces. This lacuna is a direct threat to critical thinking, and so has clear implications for democracy.

The Role of the Public

In 1925, Walter Lippmann, an American journalist and social commentator, published *The Phantom Public*.[12] It was a critique of the central tenet of the liberal democratic system—once the barriers to freedom are taken away, an active and intelligent public will act as a sovereign. In a time marked with low voter turnouts and apathy, Lippmann refused to blame the citizens for not voting in elections and informing themselves by following speeches and public documents. He believed that the public had been saddled with an impossible task to achieve an unattainable ideal. Lippmann's main argument was that the basic assumptions of the democratic theory were unfounded. The democratic theory holds that citizens are able to come together as an informed collective to make decisions that will benefit both the state as a whole and the individuals who form a part of it. This idea prospers only if the sharing of information and ideas in a society lead the public to make logical and considerate decisions. Lippmann argued that unless this was true, democracy as a means of governance was a futile ideal.

Lippmann strongly believed that the idea of an informed and rational public, capable of making decisions as a collective, was a myth. He was of the opinion that given the complexity of the issues faced by modern societies, the idea that individuals were expected to inform themselves meaningfully and form themselves into a responsible and aware public was simply impossible. He argued that the accepted ideal of an omnipotent and sovereign individual was not met by any living individual—even those driven by and trained in the questions of public interest—let alone those whose daily business did not entail thinking about these issues. The public was not in direct contact with its environment; rather, it existed in a 'pseudo-environment' composed 'partly of fictions and partly of representations made by man himself from incomplete information'. This meant that public opinion was built upon indirect, unseen and puzzling information about which no certain conclusions could be made. This fiction in Lippmann's analysis led to what he called 'the disenchanted man', the citizen who is told that they must have an active role in the polity, but cannot find the time, does not understand the issues, and is frankly not interested. As a result, the democratic theory does not account for how people arrive at a 'common will' that can be called 'public opinion'. This public opinion is, in fact, created in a process called the 'manufacture of consent', a fate that ordinary people have to live with. While the idea of manufacturing consent is supposed to have existed in dictatorial regimes where the public had no real choice, Lippmann believed that it existed in democracies as well, only having become more sophisticated by drawing upon psychological research and exercised through the power of communication.

Lippmann's response to this challenge was an unabashedly elitist and technocratic one. He recommended the delegation of all authority and decision-making to specialized and competent experts—insiders who had the training and expertise to deal with issues. He argued for an intellectual elite that would apply scientific management to democracy in order to tame it. Lippmann disparaged the amateur outsider in favour of the expert insider. His solution was having intelligence divisions and social scientists to support the different government departments and provide expertise to guide decisions.

Despite strong disagreements with Lippmann's technocratic solutions, this book is a homage to Lippmann's work. *The Phantom Public*, as well as his book *Public Opinion*, continue to be relevant to the problems of how citizens access and respond to information necessary for them to exercise meaningful choice in a democracy.

Several themes in Lippmann's *The Phantom Public* would fit in perfectly with any contemporary analysis of the citizen's capacity to participate with modern democracies. The complexity of the world and new technologies continue to test the cognitive capacities of the public. There is even greater centralization of power in platforms and special interest forces that assume the invented voice of public interest. Finally, the manufacturing of public consent by strategic use of the media remains central to the discourse on democracy and information, as it was in the 1920s when Lippmann's book was published.

In a much more recent book, *Democracy for Realists: Why Elections Do Not Produce Responsive Government* by Christopher Achen and Larry Bartels,[13] the fictional ideal of a citizen as a sovereign, omnicompetent being is again subjected to a similar critique. Achen and Bartels dispel popular notions about the folk theory of democracy—the belief system that the voting public supports, elects and embraces candidates who reflect the collective 'wishes and desires' of the people. The folk theory of democracy proposes that we make political decisions by seeking information, weighing the evidence and using it to choose good policies, and then attempt to elect a government that will champion those policies. This is done through reasonable engagement and discourse with other rational voters. Achen and Bartels argue that in most cases, the public does not have access to information required to understand policies, nor does it exhibit any desire to seek such information.

The arguments made by Lippmann, Achen and Bartels are not without their detractors. The most prominent of them is John Dewey, who responded to Lippmann's critique in a series of lectures in the 1920s and 1930s that culminated in a book called *The Public and Its Problems*.[14] Dewey agreed with Lippmann's analysis of the problem plaguing the state of democracy; however, he strongly differed with his technocratic solutions. He famously said that the public was not a 'phantom' but was merely in eclipse, and that it was not naturally and structurally unable to form informed and rational collectives. The role of the public is not that of an omnipotent decision-making body, but rather, to intervene, at critical junctures, through means such as the voting system. While Dewey agreed with Lippmann's diagnosis of the public as fundamentally irrational, this was not its defining characteristic; rather, it was the social existence of the public that defined it. The public is the sum of its parts. It is not important for each member of the public to have complete information needed to exercise judgement. It functions through cooperation between its members.

Like Dewey, this book does not believe in abandoning or reorienting the democratic project in favour of technocratic expertise. The public is not fiction as Lippmann describes it to be, and this apparent fictionality is not at the root of its problems either. The forces of technology have restructured human relations time and time again, and in each instance, the public's way of accessing meaningful information, organizing itself and shaping its shared opinions has been seen to change. Simply put, the rise of newer technologies transforms how the public engages with democratic processes. The answers to the public's problems must be found in how it exists socially and deliberately as a group. In recent times, the use of social media and messaging platforms as political tools of targeting, gathering and mobilizing has reconfigured how the public functions. How new media thwarts and enables the goals of the public and the democratic project in India is the primary subject of this book.

India's Deliberative Democracy

The Republic of India is the most reckless political experiment in human history.

–Ramachandra Guha, historian

In 1947, when India achieved independence, it was through a mass political movement of the people. At the forefront of the independence struggle was the Indian National Congress (INC) which, in the late nineteenth and the early twentieth centuries, played the role of an ad hoc body 'striving for practical ends through practical means, while challenging an enemy that raised no insuperable ideological barriers to Indian self-government'.[15] The movement was about attaining self-rule, rather than a particular form of government. It was marked by ideological pragmatism, instead of strict adherence to politically committed positions. Western scholars have often seen this as the root of what they perceive as the lack of political ideology in India.[16] Despite a mass political movement, India did not witness a political or social revolution. Neither did the movement focus on overthrowing the government machinery (rather, the goal was to take gradual control), nor did it significantly challenge social structures.

This ideological pragmatism allowed various forms of political theories to exist parallelly within the INC. On one end, there was the system of constitutional reforms promoted by Motilal Nehru and Chittaranjan Das; on the other, there was Subhas Chandra Bose's Forward Bloc advocating socialism and militancy as the means to a classless society. All major mass mobilizations, such as the Non-Cooperation and the Civil Disobedience movements, were a unique cocktail of liberalism, anarchism and passive-aggressive politics practised by Mahatma Gandhi. In stark contrast to the West, political philosophy in India was not based on authoritative texts that articulate clear principles. Take liberalism, for instance. In his essay, *The Absent Liberal*, historian Ramachandra Guha describes liberalism as a sensibility, not a theory in India.[17] Leading theorists in the West were not the guiding lights for the political movement in India. Rather, it grew as an intellectual response to the unique experiences of a large and diverse region.

Resilience of the Indian Democracy

This seeming lack of regard for ideological grounding, however, should not lead to the conclusion that the polity in India is not evolved. When nearly 200 million uneducated and unpropertied people were provided franchise in 1947, it was a bold and unprecedented experiment—one designed to fail according to the prevalent wisdom at the time. Historian Sudipta Kaviraj says that, 'Viewed from the angle of conventional political theory, Indian democracy is inexplicable. It defies all the preconditions that theory lays down for the success of democratic government.'[18] Despite this, democracy in independent India has trudged along, at times flourished, and managed to sustain itself throughout its short history.

India exhibits many signs of being a thriving democracy—the constantly growing politicization of social relationships; discourses of equality pervading more areas of social life; and impressive voter turnouts, especially amongst the poor and the dispossessed.[19] Even though there is a common belief that the Indian public is apathetic, statistics from elections in India tell a vastly different story. It may surprise many to know that the elections in India are some of the most fiercely competitive in the world, with some of the lowest rates of incumbency, and among the highest voter turnout figures in the world. Roughly, two out of three times, the incumbent governments get voted out in elections in India. The index of volatility, which is the net change in a party's vote share from one election to the next, is also much higher in India than in most of the western European countries.[20] All of this would suggest that India's public is much more involved and responsive to the agendas and performances of political parties than its Western counterparts. The rich multi-party system in India, which offers the public a range of choices to pick from, is a pivotal factor in creating complex standpoints, which are not reduced to the binaries of the two major national parties. In the 2019 general elections, seven national parties, fifty-nine state parties and 421 other parties contested the elections. Additionally, there were thousands of independent candidates. There are currently thirty-seven political parties represented in the Lok Sabha, along with one independent member with no party affiliation. Only seven parties have more than five members in the Lower House.

Homegrown Political Ideologies

It is natural that ideologies will evolve in response to the political problems of the region, and this is as true in India as it is in the West. Let us take the example of liberal politics. While liberal traditions in the West developed in response to the problems, first, of monarchy and absolutism, and later, of inequality with growing industrialization, in India it had much to do with the societal inequities. Indian liberalism is often traced to Raja Ram Mohan Roy, who, while not expressly identifying himself as a liberal, stood for a lot of values that the liberals treasured. Roy advocated many issues that resonated with liberalism, such as equality, free speech and social reform.[21] He campaigned vigorously not only for the abolishment of sati, but also for property rights for women, banning child marriage, education as a means of social reform and freedom of the press. Even today, liberalism in India differs from the Western understanding of the ideology. Indian liberals never fully accepted the non-interventionist role of the government espoused by the classical liberals, and the idea of individual rights was tempered to a more Indian understanding of society aspiring towards a common good.

In India, political discussions are usually centred on the issues related to the state that should regulate social norms, and whether and how the state should redistribute private property. In their book, *Ideology and Identity: The Changing Party Systems of India*, Pradeep Chhibber and Rahul Verma called this the 'politics of statism'.[22] The other dominant issue in India, according to them, is how the state should accommodate the needs of various marginalized groups and protect minority rights from assertive majoritarian tendencies. This they call the 'politics of recognition'. These two strands of statism and recognition are also prominent in any study of constituent assembly debates, and constitutional jurisprudence on issues such as rights, state powers, due processes, reservations and federalism in India. Those looking at the country using the Western paradigm of political discourse, along the ideas of the conflicts between State and Church, the urban and rural populations, federalism and centralization, and capital and labour forces will mistakenly see a lack of ideological positions in its political discourse. These factors do not necessarily dominate the discourse in India, but that does not mean that it does not have its own issues along which political ideologies are divided.

The 'Argumentative Indian'

One dominant explanation for why and how India has, despite the odds, managed to sustain its democracy can be found in Amartya Sen's articulation of 'an argumentative tradition' in the country.[23] The popular trope that people in India gather at tea shops in the evenings to debate and discuss political issues was, in fact, used successfully in Prime Minister Narendra Modi's 'Chai Pe Charcha' election campaign in 2014. This idea of an argumentative tradition recognizes the Indian people as politically involved, despite their economic circumstances or lack of formal education. For a thriving democracy, three essential components are generally necessary—free and fair elections, working forms of deliberation and the ability of its people to organize themselves for protest. While free and fair elections are very much the minimum standard, the deliberative nature of India's democracy is equally important and relates directly to this argumentative tradition.

A working deliberative democracy requires more than a majoritarian procedure of decision-making. It must have an exchange of reasons and arguments, and elected representatives must justify their decisions through public discourse and respond to questions that the citizens ask in return. The process of deliberation, debate and persuasion, in addition to elections, is crucial for the legitimacy of a functioning democracy. For deliberations to be effective, it is necessary that public discussions between different points of view play a role in the exercise of political power.

Sen traces the historical roots of the Indian deliberative tradition to religious councils hosted by early Indian Buddhists in the fifth century BC to resolve not just religious debates, but also carry out social and civic duties. Others have looked at interfaith dialogues during the reign of Mughal emperor Akbar as examples of reasoned discourse between parties seeking rational thought rather than relying on traditional knowledge. In the more recent past, Gandhi, and before him in the nineteenth century, British bureaucrat Henry Maine, had sought to institutionalize indigenous systems of autonomous village governments, whose structures and practices shared many characteristics of participatory democracy. Maine felt that India's rich tradition of deliberative practices made it suitable for the village community as an alternative to a centralized form of governance. The Gandhian view of bottom-up democracy and self-reliant villages was largely inspired by Maine. The debates, which saw the participation of 299 members and took 165 days, created India's foundational document.

The rejection of the Gandhian ideal of village democracy by B.R. Ambedkar in the constitutional assembly debates was driven by what he described as the 'life of contradictions' in India's democracy. Ambedkar argued that despite the peculiar participatory culture of political deliberations at the village level, the extreme state of social and economic inequality (more than 85 per cent of India's population was illiterate and devoid of property) did not permit such a decentralized form of governance. Ambedkar's scepticism about the potential of village democracy in India is echoed in the works of scholars like Jürgen Habermas. Habermas views deliberation as rooted in equality, rationality and a free exchange of ideas—a means to discuss and resolve differences in a diverse polity, whether in parliamentary discussions or in public forums of varying kinds. Polities such as India, with their deep social and economic inequality, illiteracy and entrenched identity politics, are not supposed to be ideally suited for this. When celebrating India's argumentative tradition, we would be remiss if we did not acknowledge this.

Despite Sen's strong belief in India's argumentative traditions, the deliberative nature of India's democracy has been under threat for some time. Our legislative bodies do not meet, and when they do, rarely engage in robust debates over policy. The sixteenth Lok Sabha only sat for 331 days—way below the average. The total number of working hours of the Lok Sabha in the last fifteen years is roughly half of what it was in the first fifteen years of our democracy. The trend of important policies being sanctioned by executive fiat rather than legislative deliberation has only steadily risen over the years. The number of Bills referred to committees for feedback and deliberation has gone down from 71 per cent to 25 per cent in just the last two Lok Sabhas (fourteenth to sixteenth).[24]

The advent of the Internet and social media has meant that millions of people interact with each other and debate issues every day. While it was supposed to lead to a more informed public, more citizen-led forms of engagement and a democratization of the media, we don't seem to have a surge of better or more informed thinking about important issues. It has only led to superficial thinking, and unthinking adoption of ideological positions, marked with parochialism, sectarianism and racism. How the culture of untruth and rampant extreme speech comes in the way of the exercises of deliberative democracy will be dealt with in detail in this book. The essence of democratic politics is not simply in the right to vote, and in free and fair elections. It is in the public being able to engage in the exchange of ideas, and the common deliberation that can inform collective decision-making.

PART ONE
Public Access to (Mis)Information

CHAPTER 1
Making Sense of Misinformation

In times of universal deceit, telling the truth will be a revolutionary act.

—George Orwell, novelist

In 2016, Craig Silverman, the media editor of BuzzFeed, began looking into a stream of fictitious news stories about American politics. When he investigated further, he found over 140 news websites registered from a small Balkan town of 55,000 people called Veles. These websites, such as Trumpvision365.com, USConservativeToday.com, DonaldTrumpNews.co and USADailyPolitics.com, sounded like American news websites. Almost all of them published content that was wildly false and favoured the then-US presidential candidate, Donald Trump.

Their investigation revealed that these websites were run by youngsters in Veles, Macedonia, who had found an easy way to make money online. Their modus operandi was simple. They borrowed, or, in many cases, plagiarized content from fringe right-wing websites. These stories were posted with some edits and sensational headlines by the Macedonian youth on their websites. They would then share it on Facebook to generate traffic. Hits on Facebook would translate into ad revenue. They targeted American users, as Facebook itself considers them worth about four times a user outside the US, in ad revenues.[25]

In a short span of time, the term 'fake news' went from being a social media term to a political slur. Since the 2016 US elections, the phenomenon of 'fake news' has been receiving a lot of scholarly and media attention. In March 2017, Sir Tim Berners-Lee, one of the creators of the World Wide Web, had called for a crackdown, stating in an open letter that 'misinformation, or fake news, which is surprising, shocking or designed to appeal to our biases, can spread like wildfire'. A report by Gartner, one of the world's leading advisory companies, highlighted 'increased fake news' as one of its predictions for the next few years to come. The report states that by 2022, 'a majority of individuals in mature economies will consume more false information than true information'.[26]

A Brief History of Misinformation

In order to understand the recent phenomenon of misinformation, it is important to recognize that this problem has existed for centuries. The term may be new, but the phenomenon isn't. In seventeenth-century France, the term 'canard' was used to describe a rumour or unfounded story, usually sold by hawkers on the streets of Paris. One of the most notorious canards was about the capture of a monster in Chile that was being shipped to Spain, complete with a report that included a copper engraving of a dragon-like creature. The misinformation problem predates even the seventeenth century by quite a stretch. Back in the Roman Empire, during the race to succeed Julius Caesar, Octavian ran a misinformation campaign against his political rival Marcus Antonius in the first century BC. This is not the only example of a historical event around which a little digging shows instances of misinformation campaigns. During the French Revolution (1789–99), the canard about the Chilean monster was revisited, this time with the head of the monster replaced with the face of Marie Antoinette, Queen of France. This was an organized attempt to disparage the queen, and it may have contributed to fuelling hatred against her, and her eventual beheading.

As the power of misinformation at the hands of newspapers was realized, state sanctions began to emerge. In the Netherlands, the legal system fined and banned publishers who would publish fake reports in the eighteenth century.

It is useful to get a historical context of misinformation to understand the ways in which it has worked in the past, how the same themes are repeated, and how we have dealt with them. A lot of past narrative on misinformation has to do with conspiracy theories being peddled without any evidence, or silly hoaxes. In 1835, we saw what was generally considered the first large-scale hoax—the Great Moon Hoax of 1835. *The New York Sun* had published six articles about the discovery of life on the Moon. The inaccuracies and lack of scientific research in these stories so incensed the writer and literary critic Edgar Allan Poe that he resolved to demonstrate how such hoaxes could be done well. In the 1830s and 1840s, he wrote at least six different hoaxes for *The Sun*. One of the most popular was about a balloonist having crossed the Atlantic Ocean in a hot air balloon in three days. Poe's attention to scientific detail made his hoaxes very believable. Despite their intent to be satires, Poe's hoaxes were widely believed.

But, as we know, misinformation has been used for much more than hoaxes designed to entertain or horrify. The use of misinformation both by and against those with political power is as real today as it was in Octavian's campaigns against Marcus Antonius, and in public opinion against Marie Antoinette. The introduction of new information technologies has always led to a rise in misinformation. This has been clear at different points in history, with the invention of the printing press, the advent of newspapers, the rise of the Internet and, most recently, the emergence of social media.

While the term 'clickbait journalism', which refers to sensational news reports designed to get more clicks from Internet users, is new, this phenomenon is by no means novel. In the 1890s, rival newspaper publishers Joseph Pulitzer and William Hearst competed over market shares peddling sensationalist reports and rumours as though they were facts, a practice that became known at the time as 'yellow journalism'. It is generally believed that this trend of misinformation and sensationalism was instrumental in leading the US to war with Spain in 1898. Around this time, Cuba was struggling for independence from Spain. The US sent its battleship *USS Maine* to Cuba to safeguard American interests and people in Cuba. As tensions were subsiding, an explosion on the American ship provided fodder for misinformation. The *New York World* owned by Pulitzer and *New York Journal* owned by Hearst competed fiercely for producing more sensational stories, falsely implicating Spain.[27] This fuelled public opinion in the US that made it retaliate, which directly led to war.

The world wars saw frequent use of misinformation campaigns. The German Corpse Factory story, the propaganda machinery perpetrated by Joseph Goebbels and the anti-Nazi propaganda used by the British Information Services to persuade the US to join the war are some striking examples of misinformation in this period. During World War I, there was a shortage of fat in Germany due to the British naval blockade. There had been reports of a rumour that the Germans had resorted to extracting glycerine out of bodies of dead soldiers. In 1917, two of the leading newspapers in Britain, *The Times* and *Daily Mail*, reported accounts from anonymous sources who claimed to have visited the corpse factories. Even though these reports were proven to be false, they had a long-lasting impact. During World War II, when news about the Holocaust first emerged, the old disinformation was one of the factors that is said to have caused these early reports to be doubted.[28]

The misinformation campaigns have also grown more organized and sophisticated with time. From 1970, South Africa's apartheid government sponsored a sophisticated secret global propaganda and lobbying campaign. Their aim was to target key influencers in the West to counter the opposition to its apartheid policies. This was an organized campaign carried out by an organization called the International Association for Cooperation and Development in Southern Africa, or ACODA, after the French version of its name. It held conferences, organized seminars and hosted dinner receptions involving several high-profile figures such as British and European parliamentarians.

Our reactions to misinformation have also been precipitated by extreme actions. Lippmann's critique of the press was a reaction to the warmongering propaganda that the American press participated in until World War I. In fact, it was his critique and dialogue with Dewey that was central to the establishment of several good media practices, led especially by *The New York Times*, which afforded editorial voices some independence from advertiser interests. As the case was then, there is a desperate need today to arrive at solutions that recognize the role that social media platforms play in the dissemination of news and information.[29]

In India, the thousands-of-years-old oral tradition and the lack of emphasis on bibliographical data provide an ample platform for misinformation. The immediate cause for the 1857 Sepoy Mutiny was rumours about the mixture of animal fat, particularly of cows and pigs, with flour, used in greased cartridges. Mahmood Farooqui's book, *Besieged: Voices from Delhi-1857*, sheds light on the strategic use of this rumour by the rebels to rouse religious sentiments of the Hindu and Muslim infantry against the British. The use of pamphlets and newspapers in this campaign is instructive in the spread of printing technology for news dissemination, along with being a tool for disinformation.[30] Prior to the introduction of printing technology, there was a limited concept of authorial presence in manuscripts in India. With a strong history of oral tradition, manuscripts (often accounts of religious epics and stories) were without any details about the author. The idea of a title page with bibliographical details was introduced later. Hemendra Kumar Sircar, who reviewed a representative collection of early printed books in Indian languages in the William Carey Historical Library, found that most books in Indian languages had no title page. Sometimes the name of the author would be hidden in the other bibliographical details. In the title page of *Chīstān* (printed by the Mohammadi Press in Lucknow in 1839), for instance, the name of the author is only presented in the form of a six-petal flower.[31] It was in 1867 that the Press and Registration of Books Act was passed, making it mandatory for printers and publishers to print their names, as well as the place and date of publication on the title page of every book. The practice of providing bibliographical data and its contents became crystallized only after this. The practice of limited bibliographical data continued in the forms of pamphlets and even newspaper reports, and one sees a correlation between the lack of author details and the use of the medium for misinformation.

What Do We Mean by Misinformation?

The debate around misinformation often pays little heed to the semantics of the term, and how we understand it. To begin with, the term 'fake news' was used to refer to a satire on political news, and early commentary was concerned with the notion that it may be becoming the primary source of information for many people. During the 2016 US presidential election, the use of the term grew, and it referred primarily to online sites full of sensational information, which, in its design and visual language, resembled conventional news stories. Then, gradually, it began to be used in reference to ideologically ultra-partisan sources of news. In the US, the Breitbart, The Daily Caller and Occupy Democrats were some examples of such sources. In India, Postcard News and Niti Central became synonymous with such examples. The term 'fake news' itself has been weaponized today, with US President Trump using it indiscriminately to describe any and all content critical of him.

In a way, fake news was also turning into a means to suppress, restrict, undermine and delegitimize the media. Soon, world leaders, as well as countless political operatives, journalists and ordinary people were using the term, so much so that it was rendered meaningless. The term was used for all manner of information—legitimate and illegitimate, including hoaxes, conspiracy theories, misreporting, sponsored posts, ads, memes, ideologically motivated news and any information that whoever was using the term did not like. This meant that even genuine news stories and credible sources were lumped together with organized disinformation, and has led to a situation where people just do not know what to trust. I, therefore, do not use the term 'fake news' (other than when in quotes) in this book and argue that the term should not be used to describe this phenomenon.

Unlike rational truth (such as $2 + 2 = 4$), which is irrefutable, factual truths are brutally elementary information whose veracity is taken for granted. Despite this, Hannah Arendt describes factual truths as more and more under threat. She says,

> The historian knows how vulnerable is the whole texture of facts in which we spend our daily life; it is always in danger of being perforated by single lies or torn to shreds by the organized lying of groups, nations or classes, or denied and distorted, often carefully covered up by reams of falsehoods or simply allowed to fall into oblivion...since the liar is free to fashion his 'facts' to fit the profit and pleasure, or even the mere expectations, of his audience, the chances are that he will be more persuasive than the truth-teller.[32]

Let us take the example of the strategies employed by Big Tobacco in the US. Despite there being scientific proof of the health effects of smoking and its direct links to cancer, it was able to fend off regulation, litigation and the perception that its products were fatal for decades. In organized campaigns, indisputable facts are disputed, and unquestionable sources are questioned. The kind of strategies used by Big Tobacco became examples for other campaigns. They first complicated the question and funded research to show how cancer could have several causes, and that there were doubts about the definitive link between cancer and smoking. Then, they questioned the legitimacy of genuine research and stories, dismissing them as anecdotal; epidemiological studies were simply statistics, and studies involving animals irrelevant. Misinformation plays an active role in raising questions over the legitimacy and value of institutions, expert opinion and the very concept of objective truth. This contributes to the growing inability of the public to engage with each other on the basis of rational facts.

Even before we look for solutions, we must first address the fact that there is no clarity in defining misinformation. The most prominent taxonomy amongst them is by author and professor of social media studies, Fabio Giglietto, and his associates, according to which there are four types of propagations.[33] Their model focused on the process in which misleading information spreads. First, there is pure misinformation, where both the author and the propagator believe the information to be true, when, in fact, it is false. Then, there are cases of misinformation propagated through disinformation, where the information is initially thought to be true but is shared by a propagator knowing it to be false. There are also cases of disinformation propagated through misinformation, where the author is aware of the falsity of the information, but the propagator shares it, believing it to be true. Finally, there is pure disinformation, where both the author and the propagator share the information with the full knowledge that it is false. These terms draw a distinction between the terms misinformation and disinformation, and the intentions of the author and the propagator.

In a 2017 report for the Council of Europe, Hossein Derakhshan and Clair Wardle suggested using the term 'malinformation' to describe 'information that is based on reality, used to inflict harm on a person, organization or country'.[34] Media historian Caroline Jack, on the other hand, argued that the term 'problematic information' works better than the terms 'fake news' or 'misinformation'. This is because terms such as 'misinformation, disinformation' and 'malinformation' are based on the intent of the creator. So, misinformation is unintentionally incorrect, whereas disinformation is intentionally incorrect. Given the ambivalent nature of content on the web and the high potential for remixing and editing, it is often very hard to determine where a particular post or meme originated, making it that much harder to determine the intent of the author.[35]

At the outset, we must distinguish between misinformation and satire, parody and other forms of ironic content that seek to draw attention to issues by intentionally and humorously exaggerating them, often to absurd extents. Satire and parody have long been important instruments for both entertainment, and social and political commentary. Online portals such as FakingNews.com and UnrealTimes.com, and Facebook pages such as 'Humans of Hindutva' became some of the biggest aggregators of online satire, spoof and parody in India. Such material has no intention to disinform, but rather, are important tools to highlight existing issues by drawing attention to them by means of humour. What follows is a set of criteria through which we can see and understand the different kinds of misinformation we are faced with in India. I have tried to classify misinformation based on the nature and kind of content, and manner in which such news is 'fake'.

Manufactured Primary Information

The nature of information can be broadly classified into primary and secondary information. Primary information is essentially the primary subject of a news article, for instance, statements made by persons, laws and regulations, reports and papers, and raw footage or photographs featured in news pieces. Secondary information, on the hand, is the information, description or analysis of the primary content. A case of manufactured primary content would include instances where the entire premise on which an argument is based is patently false.

For instance, in August 2017, Republic TV reported that electricity had been cut off in Jama Masjid in New Delhi for non-payment of bills. This was based on a piece of false news carried by the right-wing website Postcard News.[36] Such instances are usually a result of poor journalism and fact-checking, where media houses do not seek sufficient verification before reporting.

There are also several examples of entirely manufactured news reports, often circulated in the form of small infographics full of data to build trust. While building the brand of political leaders, these methods have been employed in India. In 2018, AltNews, one of the leading fact-checking websites in India, pointed towards various statements by industry leaders praising Prime Minister (PM) Modi, which were being reported in the media. They reached out to those to whom the comments were attributed, such as Philip Kotler, a marketing consultant, and Louise Richardson, an academic at the University of Oxford. Both of them denied ever having made any such statement.[37] Such reports go a long way in creating a perception about widespread recognition received by a leader. Another report quoted a bureaucrat as saying that PM Modi works eighteen–twenty hours a day.[38] Other reports stating that PM Modi had been declared the best prime minister in the world by UNESCO'[39] or Julian Assange stating that 'Modi is incorruptible' were similarly found to be false.

On the other end of the political spectrum, Viral in India posted a picture in 2018 of the former director of the Central Bureau of Investigation (CBI), with the message that his letter of resignation called Modi the most corrupt prime minister of independent India.[40] Another post by notorious website BBCNews.com (where the use of the name British Broadcasting Corporation (BBC) is sufficient for most people to trust it) had a fictitious list of the ten most corrupt politicians in the world, in which PM Modi was ranked second.[41]

It is even more problematic when those in positions of power spread misinformation. Often, this is a result of not verifying before retweeting or forwarding. However, in some cases, prominent personalities have been the origin of misinformation. During the Karnataka state elections in 2017, PM Modi, while campaigning in Bidar, said that no one from the Congress party had bothered to visit freedom fighters Bhagat Singh and Batukeshwar Dutt when they were imprisoned during the independence struggle.[42] This was not true, as Nehru, who was then Congress president, had visited Bhagat Singh and the others when they were in prison in 1929. Bhagat Singh had, in fact, been represented by the lawyer and Congress leader Asaf Ali. This faux pas was possibly a result of the lack of diligence by the PM's campaign team; however, this is but one of several such statements made without verification. The fact that such utterances can be made by people in public life without a retraction or an apology later, and that it is not even considered a cause for any embarrassment, is a reflection of the value that is placed on the sanctity of truth.

Doctored or Manipulated Primary Information

This is usually a case of manipulation or editing of primary information so as to misrepresent it as something else. This form of misinformation is often seen with respect to multimedia content such as images, pictures, and audio and video files where the content is edited so as to convey a different meaning. For instance, in 2015, during the Chennai floods, there were images circulated widely on social media, and even posted by the Press Information Bureau, of PM Modi conducting an aerial survey of the flood-hit city—but these were found to be manipulated.[43]

The early days of online political propaganda in India were dominated by pro-Bharatiya Janata Party (BJP) handles. Over time, however, as other groups became more involved, the BJP became a popular target of misinformation. In December 2018, images of PM Modi holding a jersey gifted by FIFA's president Gianni Infantino that said 'MODI 420' was doing the rounds on social media and WhatsApp. The number '420' is used to signify a fraud or trickster. The image, which was widely shared, was, in fact, a photoshopped version from the thirteenth G20 Summit held in Buenos Aires in 2018, where Modi was presented with a football jersey by the FIFA president.[44]

My limited survey of fact-checking websites suggests that the first two forms of misinformation tend to originate outside of traditional media, such as newspapers and television channels, and can often be sourced back to social media and WhatsApp forwards, where they may have been disseminated via a disinformation campaign. However, we see, more and more often, such unverified stories being picked up by traditional media. These are some obvious examples where a robust system of fact-checking would definitely help in preventing mainstream media from picking up these spurious stories.

Genuine Information Shared in a False Context

This third category is a little more complicated. These are cases where genuine content, such as text and pictures, are shared, but with fallacious contexts and descriptions. In 2017, several dailies pointed out that an image shared by the Ministry of Home Affairs, purportedly of the floodlit India-Pakistan border, was actually an image of the Spain-Morocco border.[45] In this case, the image itself was not doctored or manipulated, but the accompanying information was patently false.

Another popular use of such an image was a picture of former PM Jawaharlal Nehru held from the back in a crowd of people. This image was widely circulated as a photograph of Nehru being beaten by a mob after India's loss in the Sino-Indian War in 1962.[46] While this image was indeed from 1962, it was actually that of a security personnel holding Nehru back from rushing to pacify a riotous crowd in Patna at an annual Congress session.

Alternatively, there can also be cases where the basis of the information is genuine, but it is intentionally manipulated to convey a different meaning. In July 2018, India overtook France to become the sixth-largest economy in the world. However, a tweet that began doing the rounds shortly after suggested that India had already become the third-largest economy in the world in 2011 during the tenure of the previous government. Several people, including Brijesh Kalappa, spokesperson of the Congress party, and Gaurav Pandhi, former social media head of the Congress party, shared this story. While it was true that India was the third-largest economy as per one method of calculation, where the gross domestic product (GDP) is calculated according to the purchasing power parity (PPP), the news about India becoming the sixth-largest economy was as per the nominal GDP method. In this case, the claim was based on real facts, but there was a clear mala fide intent to ignore the fact that the details in question in the two competing narratives were not in conflict.

Selective or Misleading Use of Information

In this case, the primary content in question itself is not false or manipulated; however, the facts, when they are reported, may be quoted out of context to the extent that, prima facie, it suggests either the intent to misrepresent or negligence in reporting a comprehensive account of the facts in question. Most examples of poor coverage, especially by mainstream media, which has evolved systems of fact-checking and verification, and editorial controls, would tend to fall under this, and not the previous two categories. These could include selective portrayal of information to completely ignore or significantly downplay pertinent facts.

For instance, a news report which seems to have originated in the newspaper *Amar Ujala* was picked by other media outlets such as News18, Patrika and Catch News. The report said that several Muslim women had come out in support of the rebuilding of the Ram Mandir in Ayodhya. While the news report was not inaccurate, the reports mischievously omitted the fact that the campaigning was conducted by members of the Muslim Rashtriya Manch and

Rashtriya Ekta Mission, which are affiliated to the RSS.[47]

Such cases also include misleading headlines or images, where these are not representative of the content of the story. In October 2017, Postcard News ran a story with the headline, 'Finally PM Modi has deposited 15 lakhs in each and every Indian's account'. The story cited various 'achievements' of the Union government and made vague connections, making it look like the benefits from them were somehow equivalent to receiving ₹15 lakh from the government.[48] This is a case of headlines not being representative of the content of the news article. The use of sensational headlines to oversell, or sometimes completely misrepresent an article, is a growing impact of clickbait journalism. This is especially apparent in the case of web-born content providers for whom monitoring of granular user engagement is a default practice.

Misinterpretation of Information

The primary difference between this category and the previous one is that it does not necessarily suggest intentional or grossly negligent portrayal of facts, but has more to do with lack of diligence in fully understanding the issues before reporting. Such misrepresentations are often encountered during on-field reporting which require specialized knowledge, and often jargon, such as science and technology, law, finance, etc. In 2017, several newspapers erroneously reported that the Supreme Court had permitted the government to ask for Aadhaar numbers and PAN card numbers for income tax. Rethink Aadhaar, a group consisting of citizens concerned about the Unique Identification Authority of India (UIDAI) project, later pointed out that what transpired was merely exchanges during a 'mention' of the matter before the Supreme Court, and no order to this effect had been passed. Such forms of misinformation, while not suggestive of mala fide intent, can still prove to be quite dangerous in shaping erroneous opinions about important issues.

This classification, while not necessarily comprehensive, takes into account the nature of the content and the possible intent of creators and disseminators of content. These factors are instructive when thinking of ways to address misinformation, as policy solutions—both mandatory and voluntary—will need to consider the different forms of misinformation, and how they may impact them. Further, it is unfortunate if all of the above are simply painted in a similar brush strokes under the term 'fake news' and 'misinformation', as both their 'fakeness' and the impact they have vary.

Impact of Misinformation on Democratic Processes

For deliberative democracy to work in any manner, it is necessary that all parties engaging in it arrive at some consensus about the truth. This makes the media a vital institution for democratic decision-making. It provides a significant portion of the information on which the public bases its political choices. The exercise of deliberative democracy has so far had to pay little attention to the need to determine whether particular viewpoints are factual, partially accurate or plain lies. It was a given. However, the cognitive dissonance that one experiences when following some of the discourses in India, such as the one on demonetization or Aadhaar, clearly shows how the ability to deliberate and debate in a democratic society can be greatly diminished as a result of misinformation. Take the example of demonetization. If one listens to the members of the ruling party, one is led to the conclusion that the scheme was a great success, leading to more inflow of cash to the formal economy, a spurt in digital transactions, a broadening of the tax base and the collection of higher tax revenue. If one continues to listen to them, it will appear that the confiscation of black money was not even an objective of the initiative, let alone the primary one. By changing the narrative repeatedly, the objective is to delegitimize the original position, even if it may have been one's own. Here, by highlighting the stand taken by the National Democratic Alliance (NDA) government, my primary intention is not to make a case for one side of this debate while criticizing the other, but to demonstrate how the quality of political debates can diminish when opponents rely on political talking points rather than substantial evidence. When facts become a highly contested domain owing either to lack of information, logical sophistry or plain lies, how can we engage in a meaningful dialogue about the virtues of any policy?

The primary consumption of information off online sources, such as social media and messaging services, which do not have any filter to remove misinformation, has led to the lack of a clear distinguishing line between fiction and factual truths. There is less and less agreement on facts that are beyond dispute. The inherently deliberative nature of India's democracy cannot work if the public's means to examine arguments is so deeply compromised that there is no way to distinguish truth from lies. For deliberation to occur, the public must be able to see divergent points of view, engage with and respond to each other. However, when the facts itself are in dispute, they will only result in different groups talking past one another, and it is the loudness of voices—both literally and metaphorically—rather than any debate on issues that will determine who prevails. A key part of this strategy is to delegitimize the voices of traditional institutions such as mainstream media, experts and intellectuals. As more questions are raised about such traditional sources of information, the public is driven towards fringe news outlets, claiming to be free of 'invented' biases and limitations that plague mainstream media.

In her first speech in the Lok Sabha in 2019, Mahua Moitra, member of parliament (MP) from Krishnanagar, West Bengal, said that the 2019 elections had not been fought on real issues. 'Fake news is the norm,' she said. 'This election was not fought on the plank of farmer distress. This election was not fought on unemployment. This election was fought on WhatsApp, on fake news, on manipulating minds.'[49]

While it was rightly pointed out that most of Moitra's charges against the ruling party would also hold true for her own party's government in West Bengal, Moitra pointed to a problem that perhaps all major political players are guilty of. When the public does not have the means to access and evaluate credible information, most norms and systems of accountability are rendered effete.

CHAPTER 2
The New Gatekeepers

In a lot of ways Facebook is more like a government than a traditional company.

—Mark Zuckerberg, technology entrepreneur

India has close to 600 million Internet users—over a third of its total population—making it the country with the second-largest number of Internet users after China.[50] For the world's largest democracy, the Internet should be a boon. After all, Sir Tim Berners-Lee, the inventor of the World Wide Web, had envisioned the Internet as an 'open platform that allows anyone to share information, access opportunities and collaborate across geographical boundaries'. The democratization of information it facilitated should have led to a more informed citizenry, but, instead, what we have is quite the opposite. The average digital citizen in India maintains a near-perpetual information illiteracy about where they receive news and information from, whether or not it is true and how it is intended to manipulate them. This is, in some part, because social media has become the primary source of information.

There is a good chance that you, like me, are one of the 241 million Indians who are on Facebook. For those of us who consume and engage with information through platforms like Facebook and Twitter, the web has been reduced to a personalized, and therefore narrower version of itself. Facebook timelines are occupied more and more by people and posts who share one's own interests, proclivities and ideological leanings. Even attempts to break out of this restricted worldview by following people and organizations whose voices one may perceive as dissimilar to one's own are not often successful. It feels, in these circumstances, that platforms like Facebook resist attempts of people to burst the personalized bubble it had created for them. To me, it almost felt as if I had made a lasting first impression on the platform's algorithms, and changing that impression was going to be an uphill task.

Living in Echo Chambers?

Personalization by social media, search and content platforms is a response to an obvious need. On the Internet, we are constantly confronted by exponentially increasing information, more than we can digest. No wonder we need to rely on personalized filters to find the news we want to read, the videos we want to watch, the music we want to listen to, and the gossip we want to follow. Clearly, personalization is sorely needed; and, in theory, it is not a bad thing. We do not always notice it, and it could, in the long run, appear to be inconsequential to the choices we make. But once we start to examine the myriad ways in which this personalization shapes our consumption—especially through targeted content—it will make us question the readiness with which we have delegated these choices to algorithms.

Throughout the twentieth century, when news reporting was primarily the domain of organized news media, there were two models of how we understood the aspirational role of the media. The first, espoused by educationists and sociologists like John Dewey and Jürgen Habermas respectively, viewed media as a vehicle for public debate in which different ideas and perspectives were exchanged until the common good prevailed. This was essentially an educational ideal of the media, where its primary role was intended to be that of informing the public through vigorous debate. The second aspirational model viewed the media as a crusader for the public's interests, providing them with the necessary information and keeping the state accountable to the public. The fulfilment of either of these roles, or even an honest attempt to do so, would require independence from both political and economic powers. Despite the creation of some frameworks to ensure the independence of the media, it has been a partially successful exercise. Internet activist Eli Pariser, in his book *The Filter Bubble: What the Internet is Hiding from You*,[51] pointed to the creation of a wall between editorial decision-making and advertiser interests, as, in fact, one of the results of the Lippmann-Dewey debate. While accepting that this division between the financial and reporting sides of media houses has not always been observed, Pariser emphasizes that the fact that the standard exists is important.

Economic pressures are often closely tied to demands from the large conglomerates that own media houses, and the incessant pressure to maximize advertiser revenue and audience share. Political dependencies have always been an intrinsic part of media practices, because journalists are reliant on sources within the government for access to key information in the form of leaks.

However, with time, the ownership of media houses by politicians or businesses aligned with political parties, as well as increased public awareness about the complicity between media houses and politically motivated actors have compromised the degree of trust placed in the fourth estate by the public. Let us look at some of the largest media houses in India.

BJP MP Rajeev Chandrasekhar is among the largest investors in regional channels, such as the Asianet News Network in Kerala, Suvarna News and Kannada Prabha in Karnataka, and the national news channel Republic TV. Zee News and India TV are both owned by Subhash Chandra, also an MP, whose nomination to the Rajya Sabha was enabled by BJP MLAs. Kasturi, a 24-hour infotainment channel broadcasting in the Kannada language, is owned by the Janata Dal (U) leader H.D. Kumaraswamy. Radhika Roy, the co-founder of NDTV, is related to Brinda Karat, Communist Party of India (Marxist) [CPI(M)] MP; and one of the companies, which owns over 10 per cent of NDTV, is affiliated to Congress MP Naveen Jindal's father-in-law. While media companies being owned by politicians is not a recent development, there are today perhaps more brazen attempts to influence media companies to openly favour political persuasions of their masters, which have led to a lack of public trust.[52]

With the emergence of social media-driven news practices, it was believed in the 2000s that this was a significant shift towards greater democratization of news. The mounting loss of faith in mainstream media led many to believe that this would limit the ability of editors, compromised by economic and political compulsions, to play the role of gatekeepers of news. It was hoped that public accountability would emerge from the networked nature of the new media. Several examples of citizen journalism enabled by social media were hailed as harbingers of a new era of news.

This vision of social media as a democratizing actor was based on the ideal that it would be open, neutral and egalitarian, and enable genuine public-driven engagement. Google News, Facebook's news feed, which tries to put together a dynamic feed for both personal and global stories, and Twitter's trending hashtag feature have brought forward these services as key drivers of an emerging news ecosystem. Initially, new media was hailed as a natural consequence of the Internet, which would enable greater public participation, allow journalists to find more stories and engage with the readers directly. In 2009, in the aftermath of Israel's attacks on a United Nations-run school in the Gaza strip, most international Internet media covered the story, but Israel's home media did not pay any attention to it. The only exception to this was the liberal Israeli news website Haaretz. Network graph details of Twitter for a few days immediately after the incident clearly showed the social media manifestation of the event in the personalized cyberspace. It was clearly visible that when most of the world was retweeting news of this heinous act of Israel, Israelis hardly retweeted this news.[53] The use of social media in news-making was hailed by many scholars as symptomatic of the decentralization characteristic of the Internet.

Over time, it has been realized that far from being open, neutral or egalitarian, social media platforms introduce their own parameters to shape how information is accessed, which only amplifies the issues plaguing mainstream media.

The popular metaphor used to describe social media platforms is a curated information diet. Prominent sociologist danah boyd used this effectively to describe social media as a personal chef who prepares meals daily based on your cravings but pays no heed to what your body needs to stay healthy. The menu of information served up by social media platforms is created in very much the same way. Just like our bodies crave fats, sugar and salt, our minds also crave 'content that is gross, violent or sexual, and gossip that is humiliating, embarrassing or offensive'. Algorithms play on our insatiable desire to be bombarded with sensational content, pushing us to more polarized ends of our political persuasions.[54]

This is a new knowledge logic which, in effect, replaces human judgement (as earlier exercised by editors) to some kind of proxy decision-making based on data. There is little evidence to suggest that the latter is any more democratic in its character than the former and creates new problems of its own. Research has shown that Facebook's new graph and Twitter's trending topic, both prioritize 'breaking news' stories over other kinds of content. For instance, the algorithm for trending topics depends not on the volume, but on the velocity of tweets with the hashtag or concerned term. This means that Twitter's algorithms are disposed against a hashtag whose usage grows over time. It could be argued that given this predilection, the algorithms will rarely prefer speech or content of a more complex nature.

For a democratic society to thrive, individuals need to be active participants in discourses and not passive recipients of information. Social media platforms view us primarily as consumers and not as citizens. Their single-minded drive to appeal to our basest and narrowest set of stimuli may make good business sense, but does no favours to the cause of democracy. As citizens, we need to be exposed to more than the most agreeable or extreme form of our still-evolving opinions. The signal we give to algorithms through likes and clicks are often only a fleeting or tentative take on issues. A democratic society needs media and platforms that allow its citizens to explore different perspectives and arguments before they make up their minds. Instead, algorithms seize on our half-baked opinions and hasten their crystallization. It is bad enough that our online selves drive this propaganda, but lately, politically aligned actors are making creative use of such platforms to inundate us with misinformation, hate speech and polarizing content designed to manipulate.

However, there is now a significant critique of Internet activist Eli Pariser's idea that online filter bubbles are instrumental in locking people into ideologies. Research by William Dutton, the founding director of the Oxford Internet Institute, suggests that Internet users interested in politics 'search for and double-check problematic political information, and expose themselves to a variety of viewpoints'. Facebook's data science research team responded to Pariser. Researchers Eytan Bakshy, Solomon Messing and data scientist Lada Adamic of Facebook[55] examined how 10.1 million US Facebook users interact with socially shared news, and the extent of exposure to perspectives that cut across ideological lines on Facebook. They found that the flow of information on Facebook is structured by how individuals are connected to each other on the platform. Despite clustering of users along the lines of political affiliations, there are also several friendships that cut across political affiliations. Facebook's news feed depends upon many factors like how the users interact with their friends on the platform, and how they have engaged with content in the past on the platform. This, as well as individual choice to avoid the content when confronted with posts from ideologically divergent viewpoints, reduces, to some extent, the chances of being exposed to other viewpoints, but still leaves significant scope for exposure. One wonders to what extent Pariser's concerns are unfounded, or at the very least, overstated. I will argue later that the methods of both those who view the homophily and echo chambers on social media as directly leading to a limited worldview, as well as those like Bakshy and Dutton who seek to emphasize the weakness of direct correlations between viewing ideologically slanted misinformation on social media and specific outcomes, are flawed. They both view the public as passive recipients of information without taking into account their identities and social contexts, which play an equally deterministic role in how they consume and engage with information.

A Web Where the Default is Social

If we observe the state of the social networking market share before Facebook's dominance, we will see it was a highly competitive one.[56] It is important to remember that businesses in this space were not competing based on price. Much like the earlier entrants in the social networking market, Facebook was (and has been) free. Platforms were competing not based on price but the quality of services they offered, and in some ways, the values that they sought to represent. When Facebook overtook Myspace in April 2008 as the biggest player in the social networking market, its qualitative differentiation was based on several factors, one of which, ironically, was privacy. In its early days, Facebook profiles were, by default, more private. It hired a chief privacy officer back in 2005 and had a short, easy-to-read privacy policy. It also clearly said that it would not use 'cookies' to track online behaviour. This was a significant promise, as the privacy threats of a platform like Facebook using cookies was much greater than other kinds of websites. This was because Facebook knew the real identities of most of its users and could correlate online behaviour with the real identity of the person. Facebook also gave users the option of not having their information shared with third parties, including advertisers and marketers, by Facebook, or not have Facebook collect personal information about them from other sources. Much like Snapchat, a decade later, one of the key qualitative differentiators of Facebook was privacy, which, among others, catapulted it over the likes of Myspace, Orkut and Bebo.

After its initial years, Facebook began pushing back against its earlier-stated commitments to privacy. Companies like Cambridge Analytica were able to mine precious user data from Facebook due to its Open Graph API. In 2010, at its annual F8 conference, Facebook launched Open Graph, a developer level interface, with much fanfare. At the conference, Zuckerberg described it as a stepping stone towards 'building a web where the default is social'. The new API enabled developers to see not just the connections between people, but also more granular links between their likes and interests. An important part of this strategy was the introduction of the 'like' button, which could be used anywhere on the Internet. This meant that any website could add a like button to any piece of content on their site. Earlier, players like Netflix, Yelp and Zomato, which operated in their specific domains, built profiles of you when you interacted with their content, but with the Facebook 'like' button and 'login' credentials, that information could now flow into one place, Facebook's social graph.

Later, in 2012, the 'share' button was introduced, and developers were allowed to create apps and buttons that allow users to perform any custom action on any web object. To appreciate the significance of the graph, we need to understand how the web has evolved over the last two decades, and how we have measured engagement, and, consequently, the commercial value of web advertising. During the early years of the World Wide Web, what we often describe as Web 1.0 was primarily seen as an informational resource, a medium for publishing content. In this version of the web, the number of hits on a page was the first metric to measure user engagement on a website, and it became the standard for measuring website traffic. This changed with the emergence of the Google search engine, which shifted the metric from pure hits to both hits and links. Inspired by the academic citation index, Sergey Brin and Larry Page, the founders of Google, created the hyperlink analysis algorithm PageRank. This algorithm calculated the relative importance and ranking of a page on the basis of the number of inlinks to the page and, in turn, the value of the pages linking to it. What this meant was that not all links have equal value, as links from authoritative sources or from sources receiving many inlinks add more weight.

The phenomenon described as Web 2.0 came about with new possibilities for participants to create connections between web pages. The blogosphere helped bring about a link economy, allowing bloggers to link content. In India, the blogging community has grown steadily since the early 2000s. When there was a breakdown of telecommunication after the tsunami in 2004, the Southeast Asia earthquake and tsunami blog published text sent from affected areas by the people on the ground, playing an important role in critical access to information. Bloggers have also played a strong role in citizen journalism in India, whether it was through stories on the notorious Indian Institute of Planning and Management that sent legal notices to the bloggers, or Dina

Mehta's blog that provided useful links and phone numbers during the Mumbai terror attacks in 2009.

But it was social media platforms that truly introduced new features for participation, allowing the creation and exchange of user-generated content. The graph was a logical extension of these modes of participation, letting users share, recommend, like or bookmark content, posts and pages across various social media platforms. To begin with, the buttons existed on the platform only. Then the 'likes' were a social activity to be performed on most shared objects within Facebook, such as status updates, photos, links or comments, all fitted with a counter. When the graph was opened in 2010, it introduced an external 'like' button—a plug-in that could be implemented by any webmaster. It rendered the entire web potentially 'likeable'. These buttons allow for a controlled way of exchanging data between Facebook and the external web, as they enable data to flow from and to the platform through actions such as liking or by showing which users have engaged with the website or its content within Facebook.

Facebook's attempts to create a web that is by default social was a rewiring of the Internet. Social buttons are, on the face of it, decentralized features that allow greater sharing of web content even outside of the presence of the platform. But the design of the graph ensures a simultaneous recentralization of the web. This is done through differentiated access to content provided by Facebook. The 'like' economy is supported by actions of several actors, but not all of them get full access to data, sometimes even when they are producing it themselves. Third-party website providers who integrate social buttons on their web pages also can only see aggregate numbers around engagement with their content and other insights, but do not have a systematic view of how their content is being discussed inside the platform. This enables Facebook to maximize its data-mining activities, and at the same time keep control over the key entities of exchange—data, connections and traffic. As a user, when I use the external 'like' button, data is first directed to Facebook and then fed back in a highly controlled way to other actors. So my 'likes' are used by Facebook to personalize content for me; I cannot systematically access my own 'likes' to use them, for instance, as a bookmarking system.[57]

As Zuckerberg announced at the F8 conference in 2010, the idea was for Facebook to be more social, where 'your calendar should be able to show your friends' birthdays, your maps should show where your friends live, and your address book should show their pictures'. Design decisions like the 'friends permission', which we will discuss in detail as central to the Cambridge Analytica scandal, also come from the same thinking. These features further a vision of the platform where your identity is as much about you as it is about your friends and connections. Any attempt to build your profile would take into account not just your data, but also that of your digital connections.

The Ad Network

The tight rein that platforms exert on the data they amass is down to its monetary value. Even when web platforms provide starkly different services, issues around data, its secondary uses and how it is monetized remain the same. Google's main business model is providing answers to our questions, whereas Facebook sells itself as the platform to connect you with your friends and interests. However, both these companies rely heavily on targeted advertising for their revenues.

Alexander Nix, the CEO of Cambridge Analytica, compared data profiling to baking a cake, saying that it was the sum of its ingredients. He claimed that his company had anywhere between 3,000 to 5,000 data points on Facebook users, including voting histories, age, income, debt, hobbies, criminal histories, purchase histories, religious leanings, health concerns, gun ownership, car ownership and home ownership. Even when this data is collected from other sources, like the household data sets built by Avneesh Rai, co-founder of Cambridge Analytica's India counterpart, Facebook provides a unique platform to collect more granular data. More importantly, it provides the ideal stage to use these profiles to target advertising and content to users. Firms like Cambridge Analytica have found it easier to collect additional data in the US than in Europe. In the US, there are few regulations to prevent secondary uses of personal data collected by private parties, and freedom-of-information laws allow easy access to public records maintained by the government.

In India, we face an even more relaxed state of regulations governing access to data. Like the US, there is no comprehensive data-privacy law, but even the sectoral privacy-related laws that do exist are weak and barely enforced. So data collectors are free to collect, process and share personal data of individuals as they deem fit. Poor interpretation of the privacy exceptions in the right-to-information laws in India means that overzealous central- and state-government departments often publish spreadsheets of information revealing personal details such as name, age, gender, address, religion, caste, health information and financial details. States like Andhra Pradesh and Telangana have taken to governance by dashboards and spreadsheets, publishing all of this data on their websites in the name of transparency, feeding the gargantuan appetites of data-driven businesses.[58] India is one of the leading emerging economies and has a large base of online users. With more than half the country yet to access the Internet, this number is bound to grow rapidly. Add to this the fact that it has no real data-privacy law. It is, therefore, no real surprise that India is the data industry's dream.

The news feed on a platform like Facebook takes into account various data points from your observed behaviour. The first is what is known within Facebook as inventory. It includes all the content available on Facebook, including posts from your friends, groups you've joined and pages you've liked. The second is signals that Facebook uses broadly as criteria for what it shows a user. Signals are essentially how you are profiled based on what you post, when you post it, where you are using the platform from, the time you are spending on a post, etc. Some signals from inventories such as comments and likes on a person's status or photo, shares on Facebook Messenger, replies to comments and engagement with publisher content posted by friends, count for more than the other. Based on your profile and observed behaviour, Facebook tries to predict how likely you are to like or interact with content, keeping posts they think you won't engage with out of your timeline. As Zuckerberg himself explains in a blog post, 'Based on what pages people like, what they click on, and other signals, we create categories—for example, people who like pages about gardening and live in Spain—and then charge advertisers to show ads to that category.'[59] Taking all of the above into account, the platform will try to assign a value to each piece of inventory. The higher the score, the more likely you are to see it. Therefore, as a content provider on Facebook, unless you have a very large following, most of your content will have limited reach, with just a few of your followers getting a chance to see it.

In the US, it is led by a large number of new media organizations, many of which exist only thanks to advertising revenue they receive from publishing on Facebook. This is less true for other countries, as revenues for views per ad are usually much lower outside of the US. So, while in countries like the US, Facebook was able to overcome the barriers of entry to the news industry, and also turn a profit, in countries like India, it did not offer the same kind of monetary advantages. What it did offer, however, for those with surplus revenue, was a new model of engagement. This new model, while limited to only those on Facebook (the number is rapidly growing), gave them more insight than any other system of data collection on these users. Even for media houses, the clickbait economy means that producing content which evokes anger, ridicule, outrage and mobocracy have more significant rewards.

Both the technical architecture of social media and the manner in which it has come to be used raises serious questions over whether it creates a speech environment, which John Stuart Mill described as a 'marketplace of ideas'. In that marketplace, everyone had the opportunity to speak, and this would lead to arguments for and against an issue which could inform the decision-making of the public. But on social media, unlike public forums where you also encounter contrary opinions, the information architecture is designed to show information which an individual may find most engaging, to serve the advertiser interest.

PART TWO
The Irrational Public

CHAPTER 3
WhatsApp's Misinformation Menace

There are two kinds of problems with rumour spread over WhatsApp: one is disinformation and the other is incitement to violence.

—Chinmayi Arun

By February 2018, WhatsApp had a user base of over one and a half billion, making it the most popular messaging service in the world.[60] WhatsApp has grown in multiple countries, including Brazil and India, and large parts of Europe such as France and the UK. In India, it has emerged as the default service to connect with people and share information.

While the attention in the West has primarily been on Facebook and Twitter as disseminators of misinformation, in India (much like Brazil and China), messaging services such as WhatsApp play a dominant role. The growth of the Internet in India has been hand-in-hand with the availability of multimedia content. Indian users are in the habit of consuming information in non-textual formats. WhatsApp forwards in the form of image and video files have emerged as one of the key modes of dissemination of information and news. Out of India's roughly 500 million Internet users, there are over 200 million monthly active users on WhatsApp.[61] The number of monthly users of WhatsApp in India on an average surpassed that of Facebook in September 2018. A large amount of misinformation on WhatsApp is in the form of misleading images and videos—often with a text blurb. This is so as to make it more consumable for a maximum number of people. Gratuitous videos and images designed to appeal to the raw emotions of people can be much more visceral than text messages. They are often also amenable to be remixed with false contexts and messaging that may have little to do with the actual image or video.

Death by WhatsApp?

In May 2017, Rukmani, a sixty-five-year-old woman, was travelling to a temple town in Tamil Nadu along with four family members in their car. When they stopped on the way for directions, an elderly woman grew suspicious of them, and immediately called her son. She had seen them give chocolates to two children playing near the road. Rukmani and her family became uneasy and decided to drive back. But by the time they reached the next village, the woman and her son had alerted others and a large crowd was waiting for them. These villagers had seen videos of child trafficking on WhatsApp and questioned them about their intentions. Even though Rukmani and her family pleaded that they were simply visiting their family temple, the mob was unconvinced. They were stripped naked, and beaten with iron and wooden sticks. Those who lay in wait in the crowd also made videos of the attack, which soon went viral. The entire family was left for dead, their car was crushed and all their belongings were stolen. Rukmani died on the spot from her injuries while the others survived.[62]

This was not an isolated, random incident, but several stories of lynching of this nature emerged from across the country. While researching for this book, I was able to find fifty-six similar documented instances in 2017–18 of lynching due to suspicions of child abduction. These were instances reported only in print and online English news reports, and the actual numbers may be higher. The mob sizes in these cases ranged from anywhere between a small group of fifteen to a large crowd of 2,000 people. The victims have been disparate. While Rukmani was a 65-year-old woman innocently offering sweets to two children, others included tourists passing through a village in Karnataka, a man who unknowingly entered a mango orchard, a transgender person in Hyderabad, another man aimlessly wandering around in Tamil Nadu, a small group of tourists in the interiors of Maharashtra, and two men who had stopped their motorcycle to ask for directions in Assam. These documented instances are from sixteen states in India: Madhya Pradesh, West Bengal, Bihar, Karnataka, Assam, Tamil Nadu, Chhattisgarh, Gujarat, Tripura, Maharashtra, Odisha, Telangana, Andhra Pradesh, Jharkhand, Kerala and Rajasthan.

The videos, whose origins were impossible to trace due to the end-to-end encrypted nature of WhatsApp messages, usually involved footage of a supposed abductor, in some cases a Muslim woman in a burqa—or playing to similar religious or regional prejudices—grabbing a child and walking away. Other videos featured images of mutilated children warning about an organ-harvesting racket. These messages preyed on people's fears about their children, and used gratuitous images and videos to shock and terrify. A common thread that can be seen running through most of such videos and images is that they systematically manipulate people's existing fears about outsiders, migrants and tourists, and are strategically edited to capitalize on existing prejudices in the community, creating a tense situation rendering visitors travelling there unsafe. When an individual in the vicinity was suspected of being a child abductor, people would often forward these false messages to large WhatsApp groups, some with more than a hundred participants, and mobs would gather quickly, leaving the local law enforcement with little time to respond. In Tamil Nadu, for instance, before Rukmani and her family had visited the area, the local police had even patrolled the villages the previous week and warned residents about spurious videos, urging them to not believe them.[63] Their efforts to educate and pre-empt were no match for the viciousness of the rumours that spread with great speed on WhatsApp.

The videos were often circulated in parts of the country where people had limited literacy and relied primarily on images or video content received on messaging apps. Pranav Dixit and Ryan Mac, in their story about WhatsApp-incited mob violence and its aftermath in a Maharashtra village called Rainpada, highlight the reasons for people's dependency on WhatsApp.[64] Most people in Rainpada could not read. There was little or no access to newspapers or television. Often, those in the village would receive videos and forwards from youngsters who had left the village for bigger cities in search of education and employment. Like in other places with similar connectivity, WhatsApp emerged as the primary source of information and updates on the world at large.

Investigations by news agencies revealed that some of the child-abduction photos circulated on WhatsApp were not even from India. One of them was shot in Syria following a chemical-weapons attack. Another image of a dead child taken from a second WhatsApp video was traced to a fringe conspiracy theory blog warning about a flesh-eating monster stalking Indian villages in July 2017. Another video of a burqa-clad woman was from Pakistan. Yet, they ostensibly led to over fifty deaths in a span of six months in different parts of the country.

The strategic leveraging of community prejudices and identity markers demonstrated how the same video appealing to the universal interest of protecting one's children was used to target different kinds of groups in the country. The identity markers of those attacked across the different incidents shows how, with minor tweaks in the videos, the targets changed based on religion (in one of the attacks, the targets were primarily Muslim men[65]), social prejudices (one of the victims suffered from a mental disability,[66] another was perceived as dangerous owing to his long dreadlocks[67]), class (victims included people from disadvantaged classes such as beggars,[68] migrant labourers[69] and autorickshaw drivers[70]) and disadvantaged tribes (the Pardhi nomadic tribe, the Gosavi tribe[71]). The identities of the victims demonstrate the manipulation of existing social prejudices, and in these specific cases, particularly the victims' distinction from their aggressors and a lack of power that inevitably follows such 'othering'.

From Online Speech to Real-world Violence

This is not the first time rumours on a messaging service has led to violence in India. In 2012, people from Northeast India were targeted with violence in different parts of the country, including Mumbai, Pune and Chennai. Following this, there were rumours on messaging services of widespread attacks planned in Bangalore (now Bengaluru) on students and professionals from the Northeast, which led to about 30,000 people fleeing the city in a month.[72] The riots in Muzaffarnagar in 2013 were attributed to rumours on Facebook, and the lynching of Mohsin Shaikh in 2014 was connected to the spreading of rumours of cow slaughter on WhatsApp.[73]

These are not simply instances of misinformation, but of incitement to violence. Legal researcher and assistant professor of law at the National Law University in Delhi, Chinmayi Arun, has made the very valid but often-ignored point that even though most of these attacks were based on false information, it was not the false information that made them horrifying, but the ensuing violence caused as a result.[74] This is very different from organized misinformation used by political parties during elections, which is essentially a problem of the technological (and non-technological) spread of misinformation, and that of election financing. Any incidents of lynching must, first and foremost, be seen as incidents of incitement to violence. These are condemnable, irrespective of whether they are based on false or true information.

Arun also uses examples to show that mob violence is often a result of how the media, local politicians and representatives of the state view what they perceive as offending behaviour, such as cow slaughter. Often, it is the colour that these powerful actors give to an incident that leads to violence. Here, the role played by law enforcement and politicians in encouraging or condoning such acts of violence lends them legitimacy, or at least some measure of normalcy, whereas they should have been seen as the horrific acts that they are. In July 2017, Union Minister Jayant Sinha welcomed eight men to his residence with garlands and sweets. These men had just been released on bail in an ongoing lawsuit before the Jharkhand High Court against a lower court's conviction order against them in a murder-by-lynching case.[75] Actions such as this go a long way in normalizing acts of violence.

To pretend that such violence is brought about only by the advent of social media or messaging services and not by deep-rooted societal problems, often worsened by those tasked with making it better, would be a grave mistake. Cases of lynching due to child-abduction rumours and the lack of faith of the local population in the state protection and local police are significant factors in the suspicion and distrust that rise to the level of organized mob violence. What we must do, instead, is turn our attention to aspects of the falseness of information that are fundamental to such violence. The very nature of these rumours is that they are intended to spread—and there are unique features in WhatsApp that render it a suitable medium.

How Information Spreads on WhatsApp

Misinformation and extreme speech spread on both social media and WhatsApp, but there is a marked difference in user behaviour on the two platforms. While on a social media platform like Facebook, the content we see is mediated by its algorithms, WhatsApp offers an altogether different experience—all messages are shown, with the recent one first. Our actions and responses on Facebook are also mediated by the design of the platform—you are expected to leave a comment on a post, share it or react using emojis. WhatsApp doesn't shape interactions in the same way. In a WhatsApp group, we see a stream of messages from different members, and it is up to us how we engage. Norms and practices on WhatsApp have evolved without any personalized algorithmic training. Each group has its own shared identity and purpose, and violating that tacit or express purpose is met with some backlash. There can also be explicit rules about what to share and what not to share in groups, with group administrators playing an active role in weeding out those who breach these rules, and members policing content that they feel does not belong there. This aspect of WhatsApp groups may be reminiscent of tightly monitored forum discussions in the first decade of the web. On a group with extended family members, good-morning messages, jokes or entertaining forwards may be kosher, but messages against the political persuasion of the group could be unwelcome. Messages and forwards sent to one group do not necessarily find easy mobility to other groups, and people are acutely conscious of which messages belong where. Groups might have their own codes of conduct, but WhatsApp offered no recourse to receiving abuse or flagging misinformation as late as 2018. In September 2018, they appointed a single grievance officer for India, who can be contacted for concerns and complaints. The grievance officer cannot be contacted via WhatsApp, and a digital signature is required to reach them over email.[76] This results in an unchecked, free flow of any misinformation that a group wants to perpetuate.

Unlike Facebook—which is now more and more a broadcasting medium—where you can easily post something that reaches a large number of people, on WhatsApp you have much less control and visibility of the spread of information, as you can only see what is happening in your groups. It is also not easy to post the same message or forward to all your groups or contacts, as you need to send it individually to each group or person. Therefore, while messages do become viral on WhatsApp, it is much harder to manage or monitor its virality. It is this aspect of WhatsApp that makes it easier to mobilize. While WhatsApp is not the ideal medium for easy spreading of information over large regions, it can mobilize people in the same group very quickly. It is not as if the former is impossible or not being done, but that requires organized and coordinated effort across the cadre of a large political party. On the other hand, using WhatsApp to spread rumours that prey on community prejudices and lead to local sentiments turning into violence is achieved in a surprisingly easy way.

In countries such as India, WhatsApp is among the biggest propagators of misinformation, mainly owing to the fact that the communication is end-to-end, on a more private level, and it becomes very difficult to trace the source of information back to any particular individual. India has more than 200 million active WhatsApp users.

Even though WhatsApp was intended as a private messaging service, it is difficult to think about it today as anything other than a hotbed of group conversations. Groups on WhatsApp are all built around common interests or associations. These could be personal (extended family, friends, weddings or holiday planning), work-related (company-wide, department- and project-related), about hobbies (cricket, cinema or quizzing) or other communities (housing complex, alumni groups, new parents). Each group is held together by its shared identity. In a recent report about fake news commissioned by the BBC, this shared identity was recognized as the key driver that made WhatsApp groups behave like a collective.[77] This helps in achieving homophily, or the drawing together of people in tight networks of like-mindedness. Shared identity, association and beliefs lead to group members suffering from a confirmation bias. Confirmation bias is a well-recognized tendency to process information by looking for, or interpreting information that is consistent with one's existing beliefs. This makes WhatsApp the ideal medium for mobilizing members of a group.

More often than not, WhatsApp groups will include people having a similar set of beliefs, and will lead to greater confirmation bias. The fact that the information is shared by a person one knows also leads to acceptance without any questioning. This isn't just limited to political rhetoric but also transcends to things like medical advice, as well as healthcare and food products.

Thinking as Tribes

Over time, scholars have tried to answer why humans exhibit irrational tendencies. In the book *The Enigma of Reason: A New Theory of Human Understanding*, authors Hugo Mercier and Dan Sperber describe these biases as evolved traits. According to them, the most defining characteristic of humans is their ability to cooperate. The ability to form themselves into associations helps them stand on the shoulders of those who have come before them. It allows them to engage in what most see as the best course of action—freeloading. By relying on inherited and shared knowledge, they do not need to deal with most of their problems themselves. Rather, they developed as societies, to resolve the problems posed by living in collaborative groups. The 'hypersociability' aspect of their behaviour has evolved as their most defining feature.[78]

A lot of this actually echoes with Dewey's critique of Lippmann's ideal of an omnicompetent public. Dewey, too, like Mercier and Sperber, believed that it was not human irrationality that was the defining feature of people, but the ability to form associations.

It was unreasonable to expect individuals to exercise complete rationality or have complete information. Rather, by existing together, they could benefit from the tribe. Yet, people proceed under the illusion that they know much more than they really do. Cognitive scientists Sloman and Fernbach called this the 'illusion of explanatory depth'.[79] Humans are very good at relying on one another's expertise, so much so that often they cannot tell when one's understanding ends and the other's begins. In that sense, the new ways of working, or new tools and technology, are necessarily accompanied by new realms of ignorance, as long as people can make some conceptual sense of how to make the new technology work for them.

Mercier and Sperber argue that the environment has changed too quickly for natural selection to catch up. However, knowing how to drive a car without learning how it works is different from voting about a referendum on a political issue without knowing enough about it. A community of knowledge does not work, as well, for political problems. Our dependence on other minds is not helpful if the minds we are relying upon have no reasonable basis. Yet, we continue to rely on them due to our hypersociable nature. Others will rely on us, in turn.

Extreme speech is much more effective when it is framed in a way so as to appeal to people's ideological and political predispositions. Therefore, it works best 'at the confluence of precisely engineered information delivered through finely targeted online advertisement...[and] strategically aimed at a carefully selected cross-section of people so that when it is presented to them in this manner, the information taps directly into the unique regional and cultural beliefs of its intended audience'.[80]

When election campaigns produce and share messages, they

hope to craft messages that will grab eyeballs. In the age of social media, that means not only relying on the campaign's resources for dissemination, but crafting the viral messages as well. This happens when users share posts, tweets and WhatsApp forwards. Most of the research on misinformation and extreme speech shared online is focused on the nature of the technology that facilitates the sharing of information. Along with the production of the content, and the availability of a technological platform to spread it, it also does need someone to spread it. However, there is precious little that looks in detail at the role that the public plays in the dissemination of information online. The BBC paper called it the 'people-sized hole at the centre of many of the research projects and papers'.[81] The key question here is why people re-share information, often spurious or objectionable in nature, without bothering to verify its contents. The natural response to this behaviour is either to paint the public as apathetic and not concerned about facts, or as naive and gullible, easily manipulated and misled by misinformation. These perspectives to infantilize the public are unhelpful when we try to understand how we receive communication and react to it.

Sender Primacy

With so much information being consumed on social media platforms and online messaging services, we often forget the source of the content, and are somehow concerned with who sent it. Social media, with its low barriers to entry, provides all manners of sources, and the distinctions between them are flattened in the minds of the users. On WhatsApp, sender primacy is one of the keys to understanding why people share things. This was the key heuristic that people relied upon when deciding whether to share content or not, and if it was credible. Given the amount of information that individuals now receive, even on WhatsApp, it is impossible to exercise any rational analysis. Therefore, if the sender is influential and respected, there is a greater chance of their messages and forwards being consumed and shared further. On the other hand, if someone is perceived as an irritant, their messages are more often ignored. Interestingly, these heuristics are not limited to any particular age or demographic, but work in some measure across all demographics and levels of formal education.

This also has to do, in some part, with the nature of the content on WhatsApp. The chapter 'Making Sense of Misinformation' discusses the tradition of limited bibliographic data in India. The fact that innumerable WhatsApp forwards are created without even the perception for a need to provide the source of the data or the information, and that such forwards are consumed and shared in abundance, is perhaps one of its most glaring examples.

WhatsApp has come to be the most popular messaging app in India, making it the primary means to spread misinformation. Running on almost all Indian smartphones and containing end-to-end encryption, WhatsApp has been used to disseminate various kinds of misinformation, which include political news and inaccurate stories on medicines, health, religion, history and science. WhatsApp is a more potent and intimate medium compared to social media platforms such as Facebook, and WhatsApp groups have emerged as key mediums for spreading spams, hoaxes and forwards. The spread and reach of this platform and the unique opportunities it provides for mobilization have already shown its propensity to lead to some of the most horrible outcomes that can arise out of misinformation—exploitation of sectarian prejudices and insecurities to unleash violence against individuals, groups and communities.

Before WhatsApp in India, WeChat was also used extensively to mobilize Chinese American voters to vote for Trump in the US elections. The platform became a sort of 'digital gathering place' for Chinese citizens, for whom the right to freedom of assembly did not exist. As it grew, however, WeChat became less reliable, since it was no longer supported by strong offline relationships, making it difficult to judge the authenticity of individuals. Similarly, in the case of WhatsApp, the twin elements of perceived credibility and a failure to distinguish between individuals, messages and official accounts have made it a prime candidate for the spread of misinformation.

CHAPTER 4
The Limitations of Fact-checking

When the facts change, I change my mind. What do you do, sir?

—John Maynard Keynes, economist

In the last few years, in response to the barrage of misinformation online, and also subsequently in mainstream media, there have been several fact-checking portals that have emerged. Pratik Sinha, who started AltNews in 2016, works with a small team of eight people, and fact-checks viral stories circulating on social media and WhatsApp, verifies photographs and videos, and also calls out stories by media organizations that may be based on misinformation.[82] Another early fact-checking page is Hoax-Slayer. Pankaj Jain, who runs it, was driven to act against the slew of fake messages he routinely received from friends on WhatsApp. Hoax-Slayer became prominent when he debunked a viral news story which claimed that India's new 2,000-rupee note was embedded with a nano GPS chip that allowed authorities to track it if taken outside the country.[83] Shammas Oliyath and Bal Krishn Birla, who run Check4Spam in their spare time, busting spurious forwards in their lunch breaks and evenings, also have a helpline number where people can forward any hoaxes they receive directly over WhatsApp. In 2017, Oliyath was already receiving over sixty forwards a day.[84]

Over time, this has led to more such fact-checking websites. In the run-up to the 2019 general elections, several television channels had a dedicated segment to bust viral hoaxes and misinformation. Even ideologically motivated websites such as OpIndia.com now have sections where they fact-check content from the other end of the ideological spectrum. The work done by the many fact-checkers is extremely valuable, and represents individual efforts made by committed actors to painstakingly engage with the ecosystem of extreme speech, and debunk myths, hoaxes and propaganda. Sinha and Oliyath both have accepted, at various points, that fact-checkers alone cannot effectively combat the misinformation ecosystem.[85] Sinha has also had to face considerable abuse and harassment, and has himself been the subject of extreme speech online, not just from unknown 'trolls' but also from mainstream media actors he had taken to task. While Sinha and Oliyath lament the problems of scale that confront fact-checkers, with only a handful of dedicated individuals working against an organized machinery, it is worth critically examining the premise behind the effectiveness of fact-checking.

It is true that fact-checking is necessary, but its greater relevance perhaps lies in the need for reform within the media. The process of information-gathering, clickbait journalism and compulsions of speedy news reporting have meant that some basic tenets of journalism, such as fact-checking, need re-emphasizing.

But to think of fact-checking as a sustainable response to the universe of misinformation outside of mainstream media may be misguided. The problems of scale have already been mentioned. But even more significantly, we need to examine its basic premise. First, fact-checking is based on the belief that when informed of the 'fakeness' of a political issue, people will change their opinions about it. Even more fundamentally, it assumes that online discussions are a form of a deliberative process where people engage in informing, convincing and debating with others. Neither of these may be true of online consumption and dissemination of news.

Theories of Communication

Our limited understanding of how the public play their role when they deal with misinformation and extreme speech is perhaps related to how we understand communication. If we follow most of the discourse around misinformation or extreme speech today, it is primarily informed by the idea that communication is like a bullet or a hypodermic needle, and on reaching its target, its typically persuasive effects are immediate and evident. This line of approach imagines information as a hypodermic syringe of messages, which is injected into a passive and homogenous population. Stories and research on problematic information routinely view the public as gullible and naive, and generally accepting of weak claims.[86] This is what communication scholars called the hypodermic needle theory or the magic bullet theory before World War II. This is a simple model of communication thinking, and considers recipients as passive. It does not give much value to how the recipients actually interact with what they receive, and how their own identities, practices and circumstances mould the information and how they absorb it. The hypodermic needle theory draws from the 'stimulus-response' tradition, which sees human beings as irrational and persuadable agents, and human behaviour as a direct and simple response to the stimulus provided to them. This unsophisticated model dominates most narratives about misinformation, which assumes that by merely spreading propaganda, political actors can automatically persuade voters.

Some instances of this theory are seen in the sharing behaviour of Internet users in India. Social media and messaging apps are full of forwards framed in the nature of public-service advisories on health, medicine and finance, which have no basis in reality. Yet they are shared by well-meaning individuals, almost out of a sense of civic duty. One of the popular forwards that was highlighted in the BBC research was that of a doctor allegedly inventing a medical device, which costs only ₹50, to cure throat cancer and help patients recover their voices! The story laments that while he is being felicitated by the world media, Indian media is ignoring his achievements. Despite there being no truth to the statements, no data to back up the claims and the claims themselves being scarcely believable, they get shared in large numbers. The mere fact of sharing of news stories and forwards that are patently false or manipulative, by so many people, seems to support the theory that the public is a passive recipient of information and will act as it is dictated to. We will discuss this example more as we look at other theories of communication.

In the 1950s, American sociologists Paul Lazarsfeld, Herta Herzog and their colleagues at Columbia University challenged this view of communication. In 1960, Lazarsfeld's student Joseph Klapper wrote a volume called *The Effects of*

Mass Communication to show if, how, when and why mass media influenced behaviour.[87] Klapper's work was a more sober assessment of what was known with respect to media influences over individuals. He noted that people could draw or infer different meanings from the same message, and based upon this, they could selectively attend to or retain media messages. This was the central critique of the hypodermic needle theory's claim that media could produce strong, consistent behavioural effects on a majority of its recipients. According to the Columbia school of theorists led by Klapper, while the media had the potential to reinforce ideas, beliefs and attitudes, the reinforcement of beliefs was largely a consequence of selective exposure, perception and retention. So, while the media may set the agenda for what appears within the pages of newspapers or that which is sent through the spectrum, little evidence supports the proposition that the media is especially effective at getting people to adopt new attitudes, opinions or beliefs. It is worth remembering that Klapper was employed by a prominent television network to testify in Washington, in an attempt to avert possible regulation resulting from the potential effects of television in the domains of smoking, sexuality and violence. Therefore, his theory, which came to be known as the minimal effects theory, was often seen as commercially motivated.

Over the next few decades, communication scholars tried to work their way from the two ends of communication theories—the 'significant effects' of the hypodermic needle theory and the 'minimal effects' of the Columbia school. If we critically look at the research, this is actually counterproductive. First, neither school of thought is represented accurately in these arguments. Close readings into scholarly articles from which the hypodermic needle theory is supposed to have been drawn shows that the popular versions of this theory are far too simplistic and do not represent what was, in fact, a far more sophisticated and nuanced theory. Lippmann and Harold Lasswell, who were among the pioneers of this theory, believed that the media had powerful, direct and immediate effects. If we look closely at their writings, they did not necessarily view the public as passive recipients, but, rather, their interest was mainly in the role of institutions.

Similarly, the focus of research after the Klapper era was to show that communication had more than 'minimal' effects of media persuasion. The emphasis of the research was on the 'size' or the 'scale' of the communications and propaganda. Getting stuck in this minimal-significant effects dichotomy draws away attention from what is actually important. It is not the size of the persuasive effect of the media that is the most important aspect of media studies; rather, it is its nature and long-term impact. For instance, if we talk about the elections worldwide, in most cases there may be a small fraction of the electorate that influences the swing vote, and convincing it may provide the concerned candidate a good chance of winning. The fact that a large part of the electorate remains unconvinced by advertising campaigns may be irrelevant to the goals of propaganda. Aside from the scale of media impact, there are several other factors that play a large role in how we consume information. With the introduction of new approaches such as the active audience theory, other factors were also addressed, such as the audience's psychological predisposition, the social context of message reception and its belief systems. These factors perhaps play a much more important role in how people respond to information.

Therefore, rather than focusing only on how many people

are persuaded by propaganda, we must pay attention to other questions. What do we know about the ideological predispositions of the recipients? Are there social motifs and metaphors that messages are situated in that recipients respond to better? Even as we pay attention to the ideological predispositions, aside from the direction of the belief, such as 'Are you left-leaning or right-leaning?' or 'What position do you endorse on an issue?' and 'How does the structure of your belief systems impact you?' For instance, both the Hindu right and the communists have been supporters of the open source movement in India at different points. However, their alignment on a particular issue does not mean that the same kind of messaging on open source software, either in its favour or in its opposition, will appeal to them. Effective messaging will need to further investigate the reasons for their ideologies. A message will emphasize that the open source software movement will lead to more homegrown 'Swadeshi' software products and services will appeal to the Hindu rights, while the communists may respond better to how open source software may curb the growing monopolies of big technology businesses.

To go back to the instances of indiscriminate sharing of fake forwards on social media and messaging apps in India, sharing of information is not merely a result of the influence of manipulative information on gullible audiences. The identities, and psychological and social contexts of the recipients of information are equally important to the messaging. In fact, to be truly effective, the messaging would have to take into account these factors. Sharing publicly is often a projection of identity. The sharing of information is, in fact, much more than the information itself, and therefore, its veracity is almost irrelevant to those sharing it. The example of the fake forward about the doctor that we discussed earlier is a good one. When sharing it, the feelings of national pride and homegrown innovation are at play. It also effectively taps into the widespread feeling about national media not paying enough attention to local heroes.

In the early years, communication theorists paid little, if any, attention to the ideas or motivation of the user, the social context of the message and the accumulation of effects over time. But with the emergence of the active audience theory, the recipients were seen within academia as atomized individuals with distinct motivations and psychological orientations. At this stage, there was still little attention paid to the social structure of the recipients. Attention also needs to be paid to the social contexts of individuals and how they rely on 'social cues and interpersonal conversation to interpret and contextualize complex media messages'. With time these theories were refined further to include elements such as agenda-setting, priming and framing as relevant to how information was received. It was at this point that we began to see selective exposure to information as pivotal to how human beings consumed the media. Also, the framing of information was seen as a key determinant of how people would respond to it. In recent times, communication theorists have begun paying more attention to how people make meaning from the media.

Even though the hypodermic needle theory has now been debunked, it continues to remain the most popular lens through which social and political commentators, as well as communication strategists, view the public. When the BJP won a resounding mandate in the state elections in Uttar Pradesh in 2017, right after the demonetization, the most obvious response was the misinformation peddled through social media about the effects of demonetization being singularly responsible for it. Some recent research on the impact of online media has also sought to downplay the role it has on democratic processes such as elections, and deliberative activities. Investigations into the impact of Cambridge Analytica on the 2016 US elections or the Brexit vote in the UK also suggest that the use of social media for voter manipulation may only have led to very limited results for malicious actors using such methods.

The truth is perhaps somewhere between the hypodermic needle theory, which assumes that misinformation will directly influence the public's ability to choose, and the social contexts theory, which gives more primacy to the public's circumstances, identities and social context over media messaging. While people's social context and identities play a large role in determining how they respond to information, media messaging is also designed to further a variety of agendas, taking into account the same social context and identities.

In a way, fact-checkers also make the mistake of imagining recipients of misinformation as politically sterilized, passive actors who will change their minds automatically when the information on which they claim to depend upon is shown to be false or spurious. In reality, the public is much more complex and responds to information as per their own sense of identity, prejudices and preferences.

The Limitations of Cognition

Most writings on extreme speech and misinformation do acknowledge the role that cognitive biases play in their spread. The effectiveness of such speech is when it can tap into underlying biases of communities or individuals and appeal to base instincts that rational pleas and reasoned counter speech fail to evoke in them. In the previous chapter, we discussed how fact-checking contributes very little to people changing their minds about an issue where they may have relied on misinformation. Aside from the socio-technical factors discussed, which play a role in shaping how we respond to information, our cognitive biases also play an equally strong role.

It is human tendency to try to avoid any kind of psychological discomfort. When we are confronted with information that suggests that something we believe in is untrue, or disturbs our worldview in some way, we experience some degree of psychological tension. Rather than changing our views, we are much more comfortable assuming that the conflicting information is false.

This idea of psychological harmony has been studied by social psychologists for many years. American social psychologist Leon Festinger's work after World War II sought to show that human beings desire a harmonic balance between their beliefs and behaviour, and when this balance is disturbed, it can cause deep psychological stress. In seeking resolution, our primary goal is to preserve our sense of self-value. Festinger conducted several kinds of experiments to observe how people retrospectively aligned their beliefs to arrive at an understanding that affirmed their decisions. Often when we fail in our endeavours, we tend to convince ourselves that we never really wanted to achieve that goal in the first place.

These tendencies get much more intensified when we are surrounded by others who believe the same thing we do. There is a strong desire to harmonize our beliefs with those around us, so much so that we may discount even the evidence of our own senses. Peter Cathcart Wason, a cognitive psychologist at

University College, London, embarked on an effort to identify irrational mistakes that humans routinely make in reasoning. His experiments led him to the idea of 'confirmation bias' as one of the key cognitive biases. Confirmation bias is our tendency to interpret new information as a confirmation of our existing beliefs or theories.

In the 1970s, a psychological study was carried out at Stanford University. The subjects of the study, all students at the university, were handed two packets of information about a couple of firemen— A and B. A had a daughter and liked scuba diving. B had a son and played golf. Additionally, it had the responses of A and B to the 'Risky-Conservative Choice Test'. In some versions, A was a great firefighter, and chose the safest options in the test. In other versions, he was a poor firefighter, but still chose the safest option. Midway, the subjects were informed that they had been misled, and that the information provided to them was fictitious. At this point, they were asked to give their own opinions on the kind of attitude towards risk firemen ought to have. The subjects who had received the former packets said firemen should be risk-averse, while those who had received the latter packets said firemen should embrace risk. Even when the basis for the development of their beliefs was shown to be without basis, the subjects found it hard to break out of their belief systems. There were other similar studies carried out at Stanford University around this time that became very popular. At the time, the idea that people, in this case high IQ students at one of the leading universities in the world, could not think straight was surprising for most people. It no longer is. Confirmation bias is, perhaps, the best catalogued, most widely studied of all kinds of biases. This is partly the reason it tends to dominate discussions about cognitive biases, as it does discussions on misinformation and propaganda. Along with the 'cognitive dissonance' and 'social conformity' discussed earlier, it remains one of the most oft-mentioned terms to explain the post-truth world.

A Model of Cognitive Thinking

Contrary to what we may expect to believe in the age of post-truth communications, people are not randomly gullible. It is this infantilizing of victims of misinformation that leads to responses that are not effective. In general, when people access and assimilate information, their psychological response can be broken down into a few steps. The first question, as we have already discussed in some detail, is whether the information is compatible with other things that they believe to be true. The second question is to ask if the information has internal cohesion—do its different pieces form a credible story? The third assessment is often about the source of information and whether we find it trustworthy. Finally, we ask if we are alone in accepting it as the truth or will others believe it too. This is not a series of active enquiries that we make, rather, our response to information is subconsciously based on how we might answer these questions.

Once we have received information that is compatible with our worldview, it is likely to get accepted, and once accepted, it is highly resistant to critical questioning. We view our belief in the information as drawn not just from the singular piece of information but a large body of 'evidence' that supports it. On the other hand, information that is inconsistent or in opposition to our belief system requires greater effort in comprehension and evokes some psychological discomfort, which can be aptly reduced to the popular phrase 'something doesn't feel quite right'. Our assessment of the information's internal coherence works much in the same way as we judge stories. Stories without internal contradictions naturally make more sense and are more easily understood. Besides, they also have more likelihood of being remembered.

If this process appears rigorous, it would be important to remember that these are hard-wired, which, in fact, enable lazy thinking. The assessment of sources is often not an additional assessment but a common heuristic, when people lack the motivation, opportunity or expertise to process insufficient detail. Then they can merely resort to an assessment of the communicator's credibility. In several cases, information from untrustworthy sources can also prove to be influential. A well-crafted story can often capture the imagination of people even when its sources are less than credible. Even when the doubts about the source are recognized, the story may be remembered after the source is forgotten. In fact, the story and source can propagate each other's reliability as well, where the repetition of the story can give legitimacy to its source in the minds of the recipient. Perceived social consensus also serves to solidify and maintain belief in misinformation.

Continued Influence Effect

The factors mentioned above can lead to a quick attachment to ideas, so that even after attempted corrections through education and fact-checking, the misinformation continues to play a strong role in the public's belief system. This failure of corrections is generally referred to as the continued influence effect. Research suggests that even in supposedly neutral scenarios, where the subjects of the study do not have any inherent reason or motivation to favour one belief system over the other, corrections rarely work. Retractions, where the previously conveyed information has been assimilated, do not have the intended effect of eliminating the reliance on misinformation, even when people believe, understand, and later remember the retraction.

One of the ways that psychologists have tried to explain this is that continued reliance on the discredited information is necessary for people to maintain their mental models. This view is based on the idea that people understand the world around in the form of mental models. Within these models, various pieces of information that they have accepted work together and depend on each other. In fact, people subconsciously look for information that can fill missing gaps or bolster existing information in their mental models. If a retraction discredits a key piece of information in that model, then their view of the world will fall apart. Therefore, even after being told, and in some cases, even being convinced that an assertion is false, they continue to rely on it to inform their worldview.

To understand how people react to retractions, we also need to look at how our memory about specific events and information works. It is entirely plausible that a piece of misinformation that fits in with the mental model of an event or an issue gets triggered in our mind when we are questioned about the event or the issue. Here, both legitimate information and misinformation are, in a way, competitors for activation in our minds. Which part of our memory dominates is dependent on the same factors in the assimilation of information that we discussed above.

Any systematic strategy to counter misinformation in India

must begin with why it is effective. Effective campaigns can leverage both cognitive weaknesses as well as take into account the social contexts and identities of the recipients. When private actors like Facebook and WhatsApp make claims about putting into effect measures to fight misinformation, it is important to understand these factors in play, and then arrive at strategies that can effectively respond to them. Having some reporting mechanisms, features to fact-check, and enforcing community guidelines have proven to be half-hearted attempts at addressing the scale of the problem. Similarly, any state-driven messaging campaign to combat misinformation must also engage with the social contexts that enable its spread.

PART THREE
In Search of the Public

CHAPTER 5
The Suspect Science of Political Targeting

It sounds a dreadful thing to say, but these are things that don't necessarily need to be true as long as they're believed.

—Alexander Nix, CEO of Cambridge Analytica

To anyone privy to how social media platforms work, the use of our digital data as a political tool against us is inevitable. But it was the events surrounding the British political consulting firm, Cambridge Analytica, that finally brought the issue front and centre globally. In March 2018, British newspapers *The Guardian* and *The Observer* broke stories about how Cambridge Analytica had acquired the Facebook data of 87 million users and then used it for political targeting during the 2016 presidential elections in the US.[88] Suggestions that this was all done with Russian involvement made the incident even more scandalous. What made matters worse, or at least puzzling, was Facebook's response—they claimed that no 'data breach' had occurred. The first statement made by Facebook following the scandal said that there had been 'access to information from users who chose to sign up to this app, and everyone involved had given their consent. People knowingly provided information, no systems were infiltrated, and no passwords or sensitive pieces of information were stolen or hacked'.[89] In India, the subject of privacy had entered popular discourse recently, when the Supreme Court had upheld a right to privacy in 2017, and the country's many Facebook users wondered how this could have happened without a breach.

The Cambridge Analytica-Facebook Scandal

In 2013, Aleksandr Kogan, a psychology researcher based at the University of Cambridge, created a Facebook app featuring a personality test called 'thisisyourdigitallife' to collect user data for purported academic purposes. Facebook's API allowed Kogan to collect data such as details about users' identities, their friend networks and 'likes', along with the answers to the personality test.

Kogan's personality test was taken by 2,70,000 people. Any reasonable person would expect that the data of only these 2,70,000 people would have been collected. But news reports famously quoted Christopher Wylie, a past employee of Cambridge Analytica-turned-whistleblower, who revealed that Kogan was able to collect the data of about 87 million people[90] – that is, everyone who took the test, and all their Facebook 'friends'. Kogan, or anyone else, could collect this data, all the while honouring Facebook's terms and conditions for its developers. At the time, Facebook had a feature called 'friends permission' designed to facilitate the collection of personal data of users without their permission (it was rolled back in 2015). It allowed developers to access the profiles of not just the persons who had installed their application, but those of all their 'friends' as well. Such was Facebook's disregard for the privacy of its users that this feature was enabled by default. This means that unless you went through your Facebook settings and opted out, every time one of your 'friends' took such a test or played a game on the platform, your data would have been collected without your permission or knowledge.

The final nail in the coffin was when Kogan sold the data he collected to Cambridge Analytica. Bear in mind that this was the first act that went against Facebook's contractual terms and policies—the first and only action that it deemed wrong. When Facebook was informed of this unauthorized sharing, all it did was send emails to Kogan and Cambridge Analytica requesting them to delete this data, with little or no follow-up. Kogan and Cambridge Analytica were not suspended or banned from Facebook's platform, and they continued to enjoy developer privileges. Talk about not even shutting the stable doors after the horse has bolted! Roger McNamee, an early investor in Facebook, who had known Mark Zuckerberg from the early years of the social media website, claimed that he 'did not believe in data privacy and did everything he could to maximize disclosure and sharing' and 'embraced invasive surveillance, careless sharing of private data, and behaviour modification in pursuit of unprecedented scale and influence'.[91]

Cambridge Analytica was a subsidiary of a larger British behavioural research firm called Strategic Communication Laboratories (SCL). SCL describes one of its aims as the creation of 'behaviour change through research, data, analytics and strategy for both domestic and international government clients'. In order to achieve this, SCL builds psychographic profiles of people, which it uses to target advertising and content. According to Christopher Wylie, a data consultant, the data bought from Kogan became the basis for voter profiles created by Cambridge Analytica for the 2016 US elections. It also appeared that Cambridge Analytica's activities were linked with companies and executives connected to Russian intelligence agencies. The notion of Russian involvement in manipulating the American public to help secure the Trump presidency soon made the whole world sit up.

In the aftermath of the news reports, Zuckerberg accepted in a public statement that while Facebook enabled people to log into apps and share who their friends were and some information about them, there was no data breach. We understand now that the collection of data by Kogan without legitimate consent was not a bug, but a feature of Facebook's platform. When Kogan collected the data of 87 million people, he was only doing what Facebook had always intended for developers like him to do. There had been no security lapse or breach of contractual terms.[92] Yet, the breach is a much graver one, and it involves Facebook's relationship of trust with its users. While ostensibly claiming to be concerned with user privacy, Facebook had designed its platform to ensure that there was no way users could exert any meaningful control over their data. It had effectively implemented a new form of social contract for data, where consent was assumed merely by the barest forms of participation.

Cambridge Analytica in India

Despite its American focus, the ripples of the Cambridge Analytica scandal were felt in India as well. The BJP and the Congress traded allegations in the aftermath of the incident, each claiming that the other was a client of Cambridge Analytica, and had used political targeting and manipulation in their election campaigns. With 241 million Facebook users in India, it is not a leap of imagination to think that social media would be a ripe place for voter profiling. After testifying before the British parliamentary committee on the role of SCL in India, Wylie claimed publicly that SCL had worked on state elections in India in Uttar Pradesh (2012, 2011, 2007), Bihar (2007), Kerala (2007), West Bengal (2007), Assam (2007), Jharkhand (2007), Madhya Pradesh (2003) and Rajasthan (2003), and also in the national elections in 2009.[93] The Ministry of Electronics and Information Technology (MeitY) sent notices to both Facebook and Cambridge Analytica seeking information on how Indian citizens may have been impacted.[94] Facebook responded that 562,455 Indians may have been put at risk. Cambridge Analytica, on the other hand, assured the Indian government that it had not used the personal data of Indians it had obtained from Kogan. While the incident involving Kogan may have had only minimal impact on Indian users, its bigger impact had been on journalistic investigations into the activities of Cambridge Analytica and SCL in India. Unsurprisingly, they have been involved in political consulting in India for a few years now.

In 2009, BJP leader Mahesh Sharma (later Union Minister of Culture) ran his first Lok Sabha campaign. He was, at the time, a respected doctor and businessman in Noida, and was contesting the Lok Sabha seat from that district. Freelance political consultant Avneesh Rai helped him with his campaign. Rai, who was a seasoned operator with two-and-a-half decades of experience, had very high expectations from Sharma, but he lost. In a detailed investigative story for the online news portal The Print, Shivam Vij explained that, puzzled by this result, Rai reached out to other experts to probe the reasons for this loss. Through mutual acquaintances, Sharma was put in touch with Dan Muresan, who hailed from a political family in Romania, and had recently taken over as Head of Elections at SCL in the UK. Muresan and his colleagues from the Behavioural Dynamics Institute (yet another company belonging to the SCL group) conducted interviews in Noida to understand people's perception of Sharma. They put together detailed insights on the reasons behind Sharma's loss, and that left a strong impression on Rai.[95]

Rai and Muresan kept in touch, and discussed working together. Rai had access to databases of households in many states. He had already created voter profiles using demographic data (including details such as caste) and political preferences of these households. He saw an advantage in collaborating with SCL to get behavioural insights and access to alternative sources of data. SCL, too, was looking to expand its global operations, having just worked on the elections in Ghana. In 2011, SCL incorporated an Indian entity—Strategic Communication Laboratories Private Limited—with Rai as one of its directors.[96] The company's other directors were Alexander Nix and Alexander Oakes, and Rai's friend Amrish Tyagi. Tyagi, whose father K.C. Tyagi is a leader in the Janta Dal (United) [JD(U)] party, also ran a company called Ovleno Business Intelligence that provided services to pharmaceutical companies. According to news reports, this Indian entity set up offices in ten cities—Ahmedabad, Bengaluru, Cuttack, Ghaziabad, Guwahati, Hyderabad, Indore, Kolkata, Patna and Pune—and worked on at least eight different contracts.[97] Rai and Tyagi have denied these reports. They say that these were projects they worked on in their personal capacities, and SCL India claimed credit for this work in presentations it made to prospective clients so they could attract business.[98]

Unfortunately for SCL India, these denials by Rai and Tyagi did little to stop the media from questioning them about their involvement with elections in India. Whistleblower Wylie has claimed that SCL India boasted a database of 'over 600 districts and 7 lakh villages', and that the Congress was one of their clients.[99] At the same time, Tyagi's company, Ovleno Business Intelligence, which pivoted its business to political strategy, listed both the BJP and the Congress as its clients on its website. In his LinkedIn profile, Ovleno Business Intelligence's director, Himanshu Sharma, listed managing four election campaigns for the BJP as one his achievements.

After the Cambridge Analytica scandal broke in March 2018, the Ovleno Business Intelligence website was taken down. According to the investigative story by Shivam Vij, SCL India first tried to woo the Congress. They worked on databases on voters in four Lok Sabha constituencies—Amethi, Rae Bareli, Jaipur Rural and Madhubani—and gifted their findings to the Congress prior to the 2014 general elections. Later, Alexander Nix decided to take on an Indian-American client who wanted SCL India to work for the BJP, without the knowledge of Rai or Tyagi. This eventually led to a breakdown of their relationship, though Tyagi's Ovleno Business Intelligence appears to have continued to work with SCL.

Clear answers about the SCL's involvement in the elections in India still evade us, but this much is certain that there is considerable interest in using social media for political targeting of content in India. With its largest userbase coming from India, the country has been central to Facebook's strategies. Up to 133 million new voters became eligible to vote in the 2019 general elections, offering an even bigger, younger and more connected userbase for political targeting. WhatsApp messenger is already the primary conduit for misinformation in India, and due to its nature as an encrypted messaging service, is largely immune to any oversight mechanisms. After the severe backlash that it received after the Cambridge Analytica scandal, Facebook announced in 2018 that it would hire thousands of more people to verify pages and advertisers before the next elections in the US, Mexico, Brazil, India and Pakistan.[100]

How Social Media Targeting Works

The availability of cheap and easily accessible personal data offers new opportunities for political profiling. Collecting data and analysing it to create voter profiles is suddenly a very lucrative business. It is not as if the methods for creating such profiles are new; they have been around for the last century in some form or the other, but the deluge of data, and its new purveyors, promise more detailed and granular insights now.

In 2017, Michal Kosinski, a researcher affiliated with Stanford University, co-authored a paper that claimed that facial recognition technology, along with deep neural networks, could be used on profile pictures uploaded on social media to predict sexual orientation.[101] Predictably, the paper generated a lot of controversy. It was an audacious claim, which critics asserted was based on a faulty premise. Jim Halloran, the Chief Digital Officer of GLAAD, the world's largest LGBTQ media advocacy organization, called the paper reckless and without basis.[102] He said that technology could not identify someone's sexual orientation. What Kosinski's paper actually showed was that algorithms could detect a pattern in the appearance of a small subset of white gay and lesbian people on dating sites. The algorithm detected differences and similarities in facial structure, and tried to predict sexual orientation on the assumption that gay men's faces were more feminine than straight men's, and lesbian women's faces were more masculine than straight women's. This finding was based on the prenatal hormone theory of sexual orientation. This theory suggests that our sexuality is, in part, determined by hormone exposure in the womb. Kosinski's critics pointed out that factors such as less facial hair in the case of gay male subjects could as easily be a consequence of fashion trends and cultural norms as of prenatal hormonal exposure. More importantly, critics felt that the paper was dangerous and irresponsible, because it could be used to support an authoritarian and brutal regime's efforts to identify and/or persecute people they believed to be homosexual. After the paper was published, Kosinski went on to claim that similar algorithms could help measure intelligence quotients, political orientations and criminal inclinations of people from their facial images alone. Soon Kosinski faced so much flak that he was targeted with death threats, resulting in a campus police officer being stationed outside his door.[103]

While being able to infer intimate details from facial traits may seem audacious, using digital traces from social networks to do the same has gained more acceptance, and has become standard practice. Social media data is turned into actionable information for advertising and targeting by building psychometric profiles. Psychometric profiling is a process to measure and assess personality and psychology against a small number of set parameters. Most of us have taken some form of personality test, often based on the Big Five Personality Model or the Myers-Briggs questionnaire. The traditional method for conducting psychometric profiling was to carry out surveys that asked questions that could reveal aspects of the participants' psychological composition. Answers from the surveys would then be analysed to create a psychometric profile of the individual or group. However, recently, researchers such as Kosinski have found that instead of conducting surveys, which are expensive and require individuals to actively participate, digital traces from social media platforms can be used to predict psychological profiles more easily and cheaply. Kosinski started out as a traditional social psychologist trained in small-sample and questionnaire research, but was drawn to the new reality of digital data collection. The use of digital footprint as an indicator of user attributes and preferences had been at the centre of Kosinski's research for some years. Back in 2013, Kosinski wrote a paper in which he analysed Facebook 'likes' of 58,000 people, and inferred sexual orientation, race and political leanings with an accuracy range of 85–95 per cent.[104] Six years before that, Kosinski and his frequent collaborator, David Stillwell, spearheaded the building of a Facebook app featuring a personality test, prosaically named 'myPersonality'.[105] This app was, in fact, the precursor to Kogan's application that led to the Cambridge Analytica scandal.

In 2014, SCL courted Kosinski and Stillwell and expressed interest in buying the data set of the 'myPersonality' app. They declined on the grounds that the data had been collected for academic purposes only. SCL then explored the possibility of hiring Kosinski and Stillwell to do psychometric modelling, but the deal fell through on monetary grounds. Eventually, Kogan used his app with the understanding that he would sell the data he collected to Cambridge Analytica. This app, thisisyourdigitallife, was said to be inspired by Kosinski and Stillwell's app.[106]

Psychometric Profiling and Persuasion

The theories of psychometrics, which guide the apps that assess personality, have remained unchanged from the days of survey-based research. Most personality tests and apps are based on a psychometric model called Big Five Personality Factors. In this model, every personality is mapped across five factors— Extraversion, Neuroticism, Conscientiousness, Agreeableness and Openness. In the past century and a half, a school of psychologists has followed the theory 'lexical hypothesis', according to which all personality traits are encoded in natural language. This means that the basis for personality types is not a theoretical model but the analyses of language terms people use to describe themselves.[107] A pioneer in this field was Sir Francis Galton, who, in the late nineteenth century, picked up an authoritative dictionary, and began noting down words he felt were expressive of character. His exercise yielded a thousand such words.[108] Galton's technique was refined by others in the early twentieth century, and psychologist Raymond Cattell brought up the count of trait-descriptive terms to 4,500. He later distilled these terms into thirty-five variables.[109] It is these variables that were repeatedly studied, and turned into the Big Five factors.

The second dominant personality model is the Myers-Briggs Type Indicator (MBTI). Unlike the Big Five, it draws from cognitive theories. This model sees personality traits as arising from differences in how we receive and process information. Based largely on the work of psychologist Carl Jung, MBTI divides cognitive functions into eight types, depending on how we perceive and judge information. According to Jung, people could be classified along three distinct dichotomies. The first is related to the source and direction of their energy expression, and most people would fall under the categories of 'extroverted' or 'introverted'. The second dichotomy is that of how information is perceived and people are classified under it as either 'sensing' or 'intuitive'. Those who fall under 'sensing' mainly believe information that they directly receive from the external sources, while those who are intuitive mainly believe information that they receive from their internal or imaginative world. Finally, people can be understood in terms of how they process information, and fall under either 'thinking' or 'feeling'. Thinking individuals are likely to make decisions through logic, while feeling individuals are likely to make decisions based on emotions.

It has been expanded further by Isabel Briggs Myers and Katharine Cook Briggs (who this model is named after) to include the fourth dichotomy around how people implement the information they process. Here, people are classified as judging (more structured and decided lifestyle) or perceiving (more flexible and adaptable).[110] Essentially, MBTI classifies people into types, whereas Big Five measures traits on a dimensional scale.

In both these models, the profile is intended to show how an individual may make decisions, and consequently, how they may be influenced. Even though these profiling methods are broadbrush, machine learning promises to find correlations between 'likes' and demographic details to find patterns that represent a detailed and nuanced psychographic sketch of the individual.

The effectiveness of these methods for political microtargeting is not a proven fact. In another paper from 2017, Michal Kosinski, D.J. Stillwell and other psychologists argue that tweaking advertising to the psychological traits of people (again derived simply from Facebook 'likes') can be effective in influencing their behaviour.[111] Sandra Matz, one of the co-authors of the paper, said, 'We wanted to provide some scientific evidence that psychological targeting works, to show policymakers that it works, to show people on the street that it works, and say this is what we can do simply by looking at your Facebook likes. This is the way we can influence behaviour.'[112] This research used the data previously collected by Kosinski and Stillwell, where they inferred personality traits such as extraversion and introversion from Facebook 'likes'. They used this in sight to target female Facebook users with advertisements of beauty products of a particular brand. The ads were decided simply based on whether the target was introverted or extroverted. They demonstrated that tailoring ads to match users' personality traits made a considerable difference in purchasing, compared to users who were shown mismatched ads. Matz claimed that this was proof that consumers responded to personalized targeting if there was a granular psychographic profile of them to guide the content. Even though this is strong available evidence to show that personality traits predicted from Facebook usage can be used to design advertising that affects behaviour, this claim has limited acceptance in the academic community. There are other studies that try to show that personalized targeting has meagre results, especially when used as a political tool of persuasion. While a fairly accurate profile of individuals can be built using digital traces, how effective this profile is in actually changing minds remains questionable.

To understand this, let us consider the real nature of Kosinski and Stillwell's findings and compare it to voting behaviour. In the book *Network Propaganda*, Manipulation, Disinformation, and Radicalization in American Politics Yochai Benkler, Robert Faris, and Hal Roberts point out that the 2017 paper was based on three sets of experiments that were conducted. In the first experiment, they matched ad type to personality type, but this did not convert into any significant increase in buying behaviour. They achieved less than 400 purchases, in an experiment conducted on over three million people. The second experiment dealt with a specific aspect of personality—openness, one of the factors on the MBTI scale discussed above. The results were much more significant for users with low openness personality type than with high openness type. Here, the results had a much higher strike rate—500 app installations out of 84,000 users subjected to the manipulations. The third experiment compared a standard one-size-fits-all marketing message with a personality-led marketing message. There was a 0.05 per cent improvement in the conversion rate in app installation. In the second and third experiments, the users only had to instal a free app, which saw more significant results than in the first experiment where they had to make purchases. Influencing someone's voting behaviour is perhaps more comparable to influencing buying decisions, which involve bigger stakes, than with installing free apps, and thus, suggests that political microtargeting may have limited success.

There are also fundamental questions that remain about such a broad sweep of classification systems. Typecasting in this manner is basically a psychological and systematic classification of people according to a specific category. One can look to differentiate between individuals based on temperament, character traits, behaviour patterns and much more, but a fairly general approach is to look for type, which is a grouping of behavioural tendencies based on an underlying and supposedly universal model. So according to the typology model in MBTI, introverts and extroverts are two fundamentally different categories of people.

At this point in time, neither researchers nor political campaigns know very much about how well targeting works at persuading voters. There is some evidence to suggest that voters rarely prefer targeted pandering to general messages.[113] And any form of targeted messaging runs the risk of being shown to 'mistargeted' voters. This could actually harm the candidate, negating any positive returns from targeting. The big issue for behavioural scientists is that even though detailed profiles of voters can be created, just because you have some understanding of the voter does not mean that you will be able to craft a persuasive message to change their views. However, even though campaigns might be unable to use targeted advertising to persuade voters to shift their loyalties, they can still be a powerful tool to contain the voters within the echo chambers of their ideology. Already, feed algorithms of platforms like Facebook show us content they feel we would like. In this case, that could be political posts or advertisements and sponsored messages by political parties to whom the algorithms think we belong. Because platforms prioritize sensational content, political agents have a greater opportunity to push voters to the far end of their ideological spectrum by trapping them in a virtual world, which only shows them messaging from one, and often an extreme, point of view.

CHAPTER 6
The Political Economy of Data

The first problem relates to conflicts of interest inherent when politicians either use campaign data for governmental purposes or use governmental power to provide data to their campaigns.

—Eitan D. Hersh, author

In the last few years, elections, campaigning and psephology, which is the statistical study of elections and voting, have become more organized and data-driven. Yet, they continue to rely on guesswork and instincts rather than on science. For example, the Brexit verdict in the UK, and Trump's presidential victory in 2016, confounded most data analysts. In India, too, the size of the mandate that the NDA got in both 2014 and 2019 was against the predictions of most observers. The Congress which suffered heavy losses in both elections, was confident of the conservative estimate of 130 seats in 2019, yet fell significantly short.[114]

Fundamentally, election campaigns need to predict the personal motivations of the voters. They need information on what the voter should prioritize and how best to reach them. The basic analysis that they indulge in is whether a person will turn up for the polls and how likely it is that they will support one candidate over the other. But they need to begin with perhaps more specific questions, such as what issues are important to a voter, partisan positions, and how persuadable a voter may be. In *Hacking the Electorate: How Campaigns Receive Voters*, political scientist Eitan Hersh points out that while these perceptions of a campaign are based both on 'gut feeling' and 'hard data', the campaign's perception of a voter's attributes is likely to be different from a voter's own self-perception.[115]

The economic theory of democracy entails that 'from the basic economic nature of becoming informed emerges the necessity of selection among data'. This immediately leads to questions about how data must be selected, and it determines what type of information is instrumental in making decisions. This plays out in both ways—how information and perceptions affect the ways that voters decide to vote and how polls, data and other sources of information affect how campaigns choose to represent voter interests.

Campaigns generally rely either on crude heuristics or on shortcuts to understand voters or on encyclopaedic microtargeting of databases. Campaigns with strong grass-roots presence can, over time, get to know the voters and build meaningful profiles based on intimate knowledge. But this is difficult, especially where the electorate size is so large, as in India. Hersh says that 'few personal connections are possible between a party organization and a voter, and even when personal connections are made, it is difficult for campaigns to ascertain a reliable estimate of the voters' dispositions'. The voter lists also shift quite rapidly in India, where voters move across jurisdictional lines quite rapidly.

State of Electoral Data in India

The most commonly used source of data in India for political parties has always been the electoral data. The Election Commission of India (ECI) maintains electoral rolls for each district, and, more importantly, for each polling booth. These are public databases that include details about voter names, age, gender, father's or husband's name, address-related information, the photo identity card number, and, in some cases, photographs. This can easily lead to inferring information about caste and religion, and profiling of a number of voters residing at a particular address, and their demographic makeup. It is worth noting that this is all legally available public data, which can be mined by anyone.

Further, the absence of a data-protection law in India means that there are no regulations that govern how this extremely sensitive personal data is collected, masked, shared, published or sold.[116] In a country like the US, the public data laws, particularly on public records that are predictive of partisan support or persuadability, are extremely important. Unlike the US, there is no organized system of registered party affiliations in India. The range of options in a multiparty system like India is also much larger. However, it is possible to look at demographic makeup in a constituency and correlate it against past voting records to arrive at broad conclusions. Where there is more data available on party affiliations, campaigns may likely focus more on mobilizing supporters and trying to persuade undecided voters, rather than engaging with opposing voters. Traditionally, the focus of election campaigns has been more on geographic-level targeting based on past election returns. However, with more granular data available, it is becoming easier to target campaigns at individual levels.

In the recent past, strategies such as the 'missed call campaign', through which people could join the BJP by simply placing a missed call, were undertaken to collect phone numbers.[117] After the 2014 elections, the use of WhatsApp was first identified by political parties.[118] As opposed to Facebook pages and Twitter handles of prominent figures, which were essentially broadcasting mediums, WhatsApp as a platform, along with repositories of freely available demographic data and phone numbers, provided unique microtargeting opportunities.

The homophily of WhatsApp groups, which we discussed in great detail in Chapter 3, provided an ingenious method of microtargeting—not at an individual level, but at a group identity level. In *How to Win an Indian Election*, Shivam Shankar Singh, a former data analyst with the BJP, has written about how a specific message could be sent to one group of people and a completely different message to a different group of people, based on available information on their demographic makeup. He says that during the 2014 general elections, WhatsApp was used by the party to primarily create a network of party supporters and karyakartas with only about 9,000 to 10,000 WhatsApp groups nationally. Later, WhatsApp emerged as a medium central to the digital electoral strategy. During the Karnataka elections in 2016, the BJP built a network of over 20,000 WhatsApp groups in one state alone.[119]

To begin with, these groups consisted of randomly collected mobile numbers that were bought from data vendors or consisted of numbers that the party collected through its various campaigns. Gradually, the parties began using data analytics to create groups based on demographic and socioeconomic factors for better targeting of their messages. Soon, other political parties also caught on.

For those who may be surprised that such sensitive data is made freely available online by the government body, it would be useful to know that the Registration of Electoral Rules requires the registration officer to publish the roll with a list of amendments at his office for inspection and public information. The ECI also sends copies of electoral rolls to political parties. In 1998, the ECI decided to digitize the electoral databases.

The Registration of Electoral Rules of 1960 imposes a duty on the ECI to publish the electoral rolls. The publication of electoral rolls was not a significant privacy risk when it was distributed in hard copies. The privacy risk emerged only after the digitization and online publication of the electoral database.

The availability of a centralized and searchable database of voters, along with their age, would allow the appropriate authorities to identify wards or constituencies which had a high population of voters above the age of sixty-five. This would help the authorities to set up polling booths at closer locations with special amenities. However, the same database can be used to search for the density of members of a particular community in a ward or constituency based on the name, age and sex of the voters. Despite some of the standardization issues mentioned above, now it is easy to write code which will scrape data from electoral rolls available online and sort them into databases that can then be used for analysis. This information can be used to disrupt electoral processes, target vulnerable communities during an election and rig elections.

Analysis of Data

Singh described how political consulting firms and IT cells of political parties would use basic computer programming tools to automate the process of downloading historical voting data, voter rolls and demographic details from several government databases online. This was supplemented by traditional sources of data such as on-ground surveys to calculate the probability of chances of success in a particular voting booth, and thereby, in constituencies. Surveys posed a reliability issue as it was difficult to monitor whether the party workers were cutting corners and faking the numbers from different areas, tribes, castes, religions and age groups, as specified by the statistical sampling methods. When the data was unreliable or did not satisfy the group distribution requirements, then normalization techniques were used 'to give responses from some demographic sets more weightage than others so that the entire set would be the closest to the true opinions of the underlying population'. Each voting booth was classified as 'favourable', 'battleground', 'weak battleground' or 'difficult', based on the party's chances of success. This was a dynamic rating, which would be updated with the continued influx of data, and would help make decisions on how to allocate campaigning resources.

During the 2014 elections, Prashant Kishor's Citizens for Accountable Governance (CAG) data analytics team helped the BJP collect and analyse the booth-wise performance of political parties over the past eight elections—including both state and national polls. They were able to classify each constituency and booth. According to N.P. Ullekh's book *War Room: The People, Tactics and Technology Behind Narendra Modi's 2014 Win*, this helped the BJP and the RSS plan in detail where to push more for door-to-door canvassing, in which constituency special squads were needed to track rival parties, and, most importantly, how to plan Modi's campaign visits. After the dates for the three phases of polls were announced, Modi addressed 196 Bharat Vijay rallies across 295 Lok Sabha constituencies during the elections. Each of these were based on the CAG's identification as 'crucial'; most of them in 'battleground' regions.[120]

During the Tripura state legislature elections, the BJP was able to ascertain that it needed tribal support. They also knew from on-ground surveys that while the tribal population were traditional supporters of the CPI(M), there were clear signs of dissatisfaction with the incumbent government. The other parties representing the tribal populations—the Indigenous People's Front of Tripura (IPFT) and the Indigenous Nationalist Party of Tripura (INPT)—were demanding a division of the state of Tripura and the creation of a new state of Tipraland, and aligning with them would place them against the CPI(M) narrative that they had brought peace in the state after years of violence and separatism. Their analysis showed that a majority of voters were under thirty-five years of age with limited memory of the years of insurgency. Therefore, the BJP pre-empted the narrative by aggressive campaigning on WhatsApp and Facebook, which was a major source of information for the tribal community.[121]

These success stories of well-managed campaigns and identification of issues that would resonate with the voters show the impact that reliable data and its analysis can have. However, closer examination shows that these success stories also include uses of polarizing rhetoric, underhand techniques and peddling of hate speech and misinformation. Another example that Shivam

Shankar Singh provides on the effective use of messaging on WhatsApp based on data is extremely bothersome. I will narrate the example below. It relates to a hypothetical case study of a party with upper-caste votes in Uttar Pradesh. It is clear that the party needs the support of other demographics to have a greater chance of emerging victorious in the state polls. The other key demographic is that of the Other Backward Classes (OBC), of which the Yadavs comprise one-fourth of the population. While the Yadavs identify with another party, it may be possible to convince other communities in the OBC category. One of the possible strategies he spells out is to instil a sense of victimhood in the non-Yadav OBC communities by playing on their perception that Yadavs are more dominant. There is sufficient data available to create a WhatsApp group along community lines. By creating WhatsApp groups with only non-Yadav OBC voters, and effective messaging about how the Yadavs have taken over most of the benefits of reservation in education and jobs available to OBCs, this narrative could soon become part of the conversation in these communities. Once this is done, the non-Yadav OBC voters are suitably primed for messages that suggest that the only way for them to combat the threat of the Yadavs is to outvote the party which enjoys the support of the Yadavs. These messages would combine the elements of victimhood, community pride and identity to position the party as the logical choice. Singh does not reveal whether this particular strategy was adopted, but states clearly that such strategies of using misinformation to demonize a particular group, and priming the public for manipulation using misinformation, are actively being employed.

Voter Profiling

In addition to sectoral databases, there are other sources of data that have become extremely popular in recent times. A good example of such data and its impact is the use of utility data being considered an excellent proxy for socioeconomic status. Socioeconomic status is a hard thing to measure. Singh reported that the use of an indicator such as the electricity bill may be useful in breaking up a demographic into a few categories of socioeconomic status based on which political content may be tailored. The amount of the average electricity bill is considered indicative of the number of air conditioners, or other power-consuming appliances you own, and it is seen as a good proxy of where you may stand in society. Other sources of data such as phone bills, mobile phone prepaid data and social media data also provide a good idea of socioeconomic status but require more sophisticated analysis.

One key source of information for political targeting in India is the caste of the voters, as several castes of voters tend to vote as groups. In several states in India, the name of the person is reasonably indicative of the caste. Some of these processes have also been automated with a fairly straightforward programming code to classify voters on the basis of their caste. However, this can have some complications. While the surname is a fair indicator of caste, often there are contextual details needed to accurately guess a voter's caste. There are different surnames used by different communities in different parts of the region. Shivam Shankar Singh gives the example of the surname 'Chowdhary', which is used by more than one community in Bihar. Similarly, there is a practice of a number of people dropping their caste identifying surnames in states such as Bihar and Uttar Pradesh, and using surnames such as 'Kumar', or a neutral-sounding second name. Singh revealed that some of these problems could be solved by having enthusiastic party workers with local knowledge involved in the tech-driven process and labelling sample data in a constituency, which would then be used to automate the classification of the rest of the voters.

In the run-up to the 2019 general elections, political parties are reported to have adopted more innovative strategies to identify its supporters and key influencers in states where they did not have a body of traditional core supporters. They actively used social media to identify supporters who may have liked their posts. They also built a group of volunteers from across different socioeconomic strata to collect home addresses and telephone numbers of potential supporters. As they built these databases, different volunteers were tasked with reaching out to them on Facebook and trying to build a friendship, and then adding them to the WhatsApp or Facebook groups of supporters.[122]

Threats to the Secret Ballot

The granularity of personal data available at the level of voting booths poses fairly serious concerns. In the run-up to the 2019 elections, Maneka Gandhi plainly said during a speech that she fully expected to win, but if Muslim voters did not vote for her, they should not expect jobs and other kind of 'help' once she won. Her exact words were extremely ominous. 'I am going to win for sure. If Muslims won't vote for me and then come to ask for work, I will have to think, what's the use of giving them jobs?' Gandhi was pulled up by the ECI and banned from campaigning for a period of twenty-four hours. The ECI ruled that Gandhi, who was the Minister for Women and Child Development, violated the rules that prohibit appeal to caste and communal feelings, as well as one that bans 'corrupt practices' like bribery and intimidation. However, this highlights a much more important issue. Voters in India who have so far assumed the safety of the secret ballot would have been horrified to realize that who they vote for is no longer confidential.

Before Electronic Voting Machines (EVMs), paper ballots from different polling booths in a constituency were mixed together in large drums before they were counted. After EVMs were introduced nationwide in 2009, there was a significant change. While a secret ballot does afford a level of anonymity, it was realized that voter identities could be predicted by reverse-engineering the voting preferences, particularly in smaller areas. Data from each polling booth in Form 20 format is made available publicly. Unlike the previous system of mixing the paper ballots, Form 20 provides the number of votes cast in favour of each candidate, the number of votes rejected and the number of votes in favour of NOTA for every single EVM. As stated earlier, analysts with a hold on this data, along with other demographic data, particularly when it is made available over several state and general elections, are able to use statistical methods such as regression analyses to calculate, with some accuracy, who you may have voted for. An independent policy consultant, Ishita Trivedi, pointed out that it is much-publicized knowledge that polling officials have travelled deep into Gujarat's Gir forest to set up a booth for a single voter. Now with the Form 20 data available, it is also known which party that lone voter had voted for. To make good on threats like the one made by Maneka Gandhi, you need not even have very accurate individual data—one can more easily estimate the number of votes one may have gotten from a community in a polling booth. It was reported after the Karnataka Assembly elections last year that supporters of the Janata Dal (Secular) went on a 'celebratory rally', quarrelling with people in areas that voted for the rival candidate.[123]

It is not as if the ECI is not aware of this very grave risk. Since 2008, they have been asking for a totalizer machine for vote counting. Using the totalizer will ensure that voting data from several EVMs are added together, and there is no way to arrive at the granular booth level data. The NDA government took a contrary stand in the public interest litigation seeking the mandatory use of totalizers in 2017. The Supreme Court also did not provide any respite. A petition for an urgent hearing on the introduction of the totalizer to ensure secrecy of the ballot in late 2018 was dismissed by a Supreme Court bench led by Chief Justice Ranjan Gogoi without even a hearing.

CHAPTER 7
The Unholy Networks of Power

The vision area of Digital India is...a cradle to grave digital identity—unique, lifelong, online and authenticable.

—Press Release, Government of India, August 2014.

In February 2019, less than forty-five days before the general elections, the official app of Andhra Pradesh Chief Minister Chandrababu Naidu called 'Seva Mitra' was reported to the ECI.[124] The ECI began an investigation over charges of voter profiling. The app provides real-time updates to the party cadre and also connects the Telugu Desam Party (TDP) workers to their leaders. However, it is the detailed nature of information in the app that drew attention to it. Party volunteers are expected to verify voters at the booth level and provide voter details such as residence status in the constituency, caste, political preference, who they are likely to vote for, and how they rate the party of their choice. The app also provides more personal information such as photographs, telephone numbers, household data, the number of government welfare schemes availed and the amount received in state subsidies.

The public debate around this issue has revolved around the question of illegal access to citizen data. The TDP has claimed that all the data available on their app is public data, which may well be the case, given the sorry state of regulations that govern the state collection of personal data. However, there is a deeper issue that exists. It brings to light the political considerations at play when elected government officials make decisions in their official capacity. These can lead to obvious forms of abuse of power, where official positions, resources and machinery are used to further the agenda of a party. In other cases, the exercise of this power towards meeting ends of the political parties are more subtle, and may manifest themselves in the form of policies that lead to the generation of data that parties need. In the case of the Seva Mitra app, it was also alleged by the Opposition parties that the TDP was using government beneficiary data to engage in targeted voter profiling.[125] The availability of data from welfare schemes in the app, though it is unclear how this data has been sourced, has raised suspicions about the abuse of public resources.

Blurring the Government-Party Lines

We see cases of governments blatantly creating or encouraging policies that translate into greater access to data for them. In July 2018, Raman Singh's government in Chhattisgarh launched a programme called the Sanchar Kranti Yojna. Under this scheme, they distributed over fifty lakh mobile phones. All of these handsets came pre-installed with the BJP's NaMo app and Raman Singh app, named after the chief minister. The NaMo app also comes pre-installed in low-cost Reliance Jio phones. This kind of collusion between the party and the government provides unfair advantages to the ruling party to effectively skew the playing field in its favour.

In June 2015, the Prime Minister's Office launched the NaMo app. The press release announced that the app would provide updates on the day-to-day activities of Prime Minister Narendra Modi and allow users to receive messages and emails directly from him. Over a period of time, the social media nature of this app began to mimic the behaviour of platforms such as Twitter and Facebook. With time, it had its own misinformation and extreme speech problems.

The app works like Twitter, with its own internal universe of content, with users signing up to post messages, images, videos and links. Unlike Twitter, Facebook or YouTube, there is no clear system of moderation on the platform, making it more suitable for the spread of extreme speech. While other large platforms have come under scrutiny from the government for the spread of misinformation and rumours, the NaMo app, which most people assume simply works as the personal broadcasting medium of the PM, has not garnered enough attention.

Aside from the unmoderated user-generated content, the NaMo app also has promoted content. Like Twitter or Facebook, users can view their own feed of posts from accounts that they follow on a feature called 'My Network'.[126] It has been reported that the promoted content from key Facebook pages on the app is often filled with misinformation. The BJP's IT cell has also said that they have had to take down several posts. Amit Malviya, who heads the IT cell, attributed this to the fact that the 'volunteers, karyakartas and fans…freely express their feedback, views and opinion on various issues…[leading to] scope for misinformation'.[127] Samarth

Bansal, who investigated the NaMo app, found several examples of misinformation and hate speech, some also by local members of the party. One of the prominent sources of misinformation on the NaMo app was a Facebook page called The Indian Eye, and investigations had revealed that the URL of the page had been registered under the director of the company, Silver Touch Technologies Ltd, which built the NaMo app. Silver Touch and its director, Himanshu Jain, had also been the subject of investigative stories during the 2014 campaign, where several websites engaging in spreading misinformation were traced back to them. Similarly, another account on the app, which is a part of the promoted content, is 'Modi Bharosa', and it regularly posts misinformation. This is registered in the name of an Officer on Special Duty (OSD), the then railway minister, Piyush Goyal.[128]

The NaMo app also has many gamified features for greater engagement. Users can accumulate points based on a referral system, if they invite others or post on other platforms using the app. There is a leaderboard on which the top volunteers' names are displayed. People can also buy NaMo merchandise from the app's e-commerce portal. This app also blurs the lines between the party, the leader and the government.

Even though it was positioned as the official app of the PM, launched to provide the latest information and 'a unique opportunity to receive messages and emails directly from the prime minister', the app is managed not by the PMO but by the party's IT cell. It also has a feature to make micro-donations to the BJP. If the government is promoting the use of this app, which is clearly being used for political purposes, it raises questions on the misuse of office power for political purposes. Interestingly, Silver Touch, mentioned above, has also greatly benefitted from several government contracts, and in 2016–17, more than half of its revenue, roughly ₹62 crore, was reported to be from government contracts.[129]

On 31 March 2019, shortly after the Model Code of Conduct (MCC) came into effect, a TV channel called NaMo TV, which carries the picture of PM Narendra Modi in its logo, was launched. The channel was available on various DTH and cable TV platforms, with some categorizing it as news and others as movies. Much like promoted content on the NaMo app, the channel was made available to all subscribers on major DTH platforms like Tata Sky, without any way to opt out.[130] The Congress and the Aam Aadmi Party (AAP) have complained to the ECI about the channel and demanded suspension of its broadcast. They asked how a political party could be allowed to float its own television channel once the MCC came into force. They alleged that the launch was against the spirit of a 'level playing field' for all political parties and asked whether the ECI had given the necessary permissions before the channel went on air. In a short time after its launch, it was widely reported that NaMo TV had achieved a reach of 37 per cent, which is slightly lower than that of NDTV India.[131]

All satellite-based channels require the permission of the Ministry of Information and Broadcasting to be downlinked in the country. Initially, the ministry said NaMo TV was a 'platform service', for which such permissions were not needed. There are broadly four kinds of TV channels in India: a) Channels operated by the state body Prasar Bharati, which includes all the Doordarshan channels b) Private satellite channels which are broadcast through satellites and require permissions from the Ministry c) Local channels which have a strong local focus, and finally, d) Platform services channels, such as local cable TV services, DTH services and Internet Protocol Television services, which are owned and operated by the distribution platform operators and distributed exclusively to their own subscribers.[132]

Unlike platform service channels, which include exclusive offerings by each DTH operator, NaMo TV was made available across DTH operators in the country. Initially, the BJP claimed that it did not own the channel or the platform, even though its official Twitter handle had been promoting it. The channel was broadcast as a government-sponsored channel and received government advertisements. Later, the BJP accepted that NaMo TV was operated by the party and was a feature of the NaMo app. The Ministry of Information and Broadcasting at this point changed its opinion and claimed that NaMo TV was an advertising platform of the BJP and not a licensed channel.[133] Even in that case, the ECI would need to be informed about it, as it would have to be included in the publicity expenses of the BJP and of the candidates, if they were promoted on the platform.

The entire experience with the NaMo app and NaMo TV is a good example of the use of state machinery to further a party's agenda. This has been so blatantly possible in India due to both the inability of regulatory frameworks to keep pace with technological changes in the media and the systematic undermining of institutions to keep a check on the executive's powers. The licensing protocols in place for TV channels are meant to play a security role. The application must specify details about the channel's owner. After receiving the security clearance from the home ministry and a subsequent green signal from the Department of Space, the Wireless Planning and Coordination Wing of the Department of Telecommunications has to allocate a frequency for the teleport. In fact, the process for receiving a licence has been regularly criticized for being far too tedious and also for giving the Ministry of Home Affairs unreasonable powers to deny the licence under the broad grounds of security. However, in this case, the ruling party did not even bother with its own clearance process, choosing to proceed under loopholes in the telecom regulations.

This is, by no stretch, a new trend, as the state machinery has been used by ruling parties in several instances in the past. The problems of booth capturing have plagued the Indian democracy throughout its short history and often occurred under the patronage of ruling parties. The most infamous instance of the use of state resources in electioneering is the disqualification of Prime Minister Indira Gandhi for corrupt electoral practices. Raj Narain, who lost handsomely to Gandhi in the 1971 polls, accused her of taking assistance from many government officers, which also included the armed forces and the local police. Eventually, Gandhi was held guilty of using the government machinery, seeking the services of government officials, and retrospectively passing amendments to regularize the illegitimate practices in her election campaign.[134] However, what is new is that due to the diffused nature of political financing as well as the dual uses of data for governance and political purposes, it is much harder to clearly identify problematic uses of the state machinery now.

Public Records and Personal Data

The tension between administrative duties and political incentives is quite apparent in public record practices. When implementing a system for the collection and dissemination of public records that contain the personal information of citizens, politicians are likely to consider the uses of these data. Earlier, we discussed in detail the resistance of political parties to the use of totalizers in the EVMs. Currently, it is easy to identify, with some reasonable accuracy, who voter groups have voted for, and totalizers would prevent this from happening. This is made possible by the amount of data that is collected and made available for political use.

Digital India as 'Game Changer'

In the last decade, a great amount of public record data has become available in India. The story of the digitization of public records in India goes back to the UPA-1 government. In 2006, the Manmohan Singh-led government launched the National e-Governance Project (NeGP). The project began with schemes to digitize different aspects of governance.

To begin with, the filing, payment and redressal mechanisms for taxes moved online. All corporate compliance gradually moved to an online portal. The applications, appointments and tracking of passports were shifted online. With time, the project began to include all aspects of governance. In 2014, when the NDA government came to power, they quickly made Digital India their flagship project, and adopted the NeGP plan under it. The project envisioned moving virtually all aspects of governance online, including the disbursal of benefits and subsidies.

Government departments and institutions in India have always maintained databases on the Indian population, but due to institutional policy, or lack of technology, these databases do not 'talk to each other'. The digital technology and a 'logic of networks' seek to create a system that enables interaction across databases. The lynchpin of this interaction has been the move towards e-governance, which began under the NeGP.

Building Cradle to Grave Profiles

When the Digital India programme was approved by the cabinet of ministers, the press release mentioned the 'cradle to grave' digital identity as one of its visions.[135] The characteristics of this identity are mentioned as 'unique, lifelong, online and authenticable'. In order to provide welfare and other services effectively, the e-governance schemes would collect and store information through the life cycle of an individual. The result, as we can see, is building databases on individuals, which, when brought together, can provide a 360-degree profile of citizens.

The creation of a lifelong and unique profile involves several e-governance schemes that document different aspects of a citizen's interaction with the state. For instance, the Ministry of Health and Family Welfare is developing infrastructure to facilitate the sharing of health information through a national health portal and the establishment of a national database containing records of citizens from birth to death. Similarly, the ominously named healthcare project, Mother and Child Tracking System, is meant to improve the delivery of health services to pregnant women and children up to five years of age through name-based tracking of documents after each and every hospital visit. There are several education-sector projects such as National Scholarship Portal, e-Learning and the Education MMP, which seek to document different aspects of school life and records, and a combination of these databases could provide a comprehensive view of the educational history of an individual.

The Employment Exchange project, which falls under the National Employment Service, creates a database of potential employees to match against employer requirements. When the e-Office is fully implemented, it will have the performance and attendance details of all the government employees. The databases for both direct and indirect taxes are already being maintained. At more local levels, projects such as e-District would be responsible for issuing certificates for income, domicile, caste, birth and death, as well as issuing licences such as arms licences, ration cards, disbursing pensions, processing utility payments and linking to other relevant government projects. They would also be responsible for the provision of marriage certificates and would collect personal data on previous marital status and religion, along with personal details about witnesses.

Alongside, the Crime and Criminal Network and Tracking System is intended to connect all police stations across the country, and allow records of any individuals with a local police station to be made available nationally. The e-Courts project is being built to provide decision and management support systems to courts, and once implemented, details of individuals involved in court proceedings in any way shall be available in the databases. Schemes such as the Pensioners Portal are already live, and function as the platform for retired government employees to register and seek their pensions.

These projects were designed to formalize the process of governance and bring about significant efficiency gains. However, one would have expected this formalization to be accompanied by the creation of policies to also protect the huge amounts of personal data being collected, review how it was being used, and determine who could access it.

However, as this did not happen, the data was handled very poorly by the departments charged with it. At departments such as the Unique Identity Authority of India, which governs Aadhaar—

the digital identity project—there are processes and policies in place for the protection of data that they directly collect. But this knowledge and capacity has not been transferred to other ministries and departments.

Various agencies in the country collect information for statistical purposes, empowered by the Collection of Statistics Act, 2008. This information is collected by publishing a notification in an official gazette, and the law prohibits the publication of identifying information unless permitted by the concerned person. Similarly, the publication of Aadhaar numbers is also prohibited under the Aadhaar Act, unless permission to publish them is sought from the Aadhaar number holder. While the legislation prohibits storing the details about religion, caste, race, ethnicity, language, records of entitlement, income or medical history for the purpose of Aadhaar authentication, this information is currently collected by various government agencies. This information should only be used for the purpose collected, but it was found that instances of caste information are shared publicly on some of these portals.[136]

Information and data leaks have been occurring in India for a long time. But with the scale and design of e-governance projects, which work under Digital India, any information being disclosed is dangerous, and its impact is often irreversible. In the context of political campaigns, these public databases present a very ripe honeypot of information to be mined and analysed. One may argue that the information was already available on the ECI's website. However, the data available on welfare schemes is much better organized, more uniform and easily mined through spreadsheets. They also offer newer and much more granular forms of political profiling as they together capture the entire range of interactions that a citizen has with governance schemes.

While the availability of public records of this data is an extremely big concern, another concern in cases where the data is not published is that politicians can sometimes leverage their special access to administrative data in order to give their campaigns an advantage. However, a more important concern is if the party in power uses the data, whether freely available or selectively available to it, to take steps that unfairly advantage it. In the Andhra Pradesh case, the Opposition parties alleged that the TDP was making use of this data to infer whether voters were for or against the government, and based on that analysis, deleted names off the electoral rolls. Andhra Pradesh's Real-Time Governance Society scheme, which is perhaps the most advanced example of the kind of collection envisioned under Digital India, has successfully centralized information about voters in the state through the use of government data and on-ground surveys. This data could be easily misused at the hands of political operatives.[137]

PART FOUR
Failures of Public Institutions

CHAPTER 8
Systematic Compromise of Institutions

The political executive, wielding the state's power of the sword, is its most dangerous branch. Liberal democratic constitutionalism has long recognized this, and made various sorts of accountability demands on the political executive to keep it in check.

—Tarunabh Khaitan, legal scholar

It would be a very parsimonious account of democracies to only depend upon an elected government voted in power through periodic elections. For democracies to work, we need effective institutions that can hold the elected officials accountable. The design of governments in constitutional democracies has always involved a delicate system of checks and balances between the judiciary, the legislature and the executive. Over time, other institutions have emerged to keep the executive in check. The effective discharge of the duties of these institutions goes a long way in reinforcing public trust that their representatives in the government are exercising power in public interest. Greed and naked ambition in assertions of power by public officials undermine the legitimacy of the offices they hold.

Elected officials often have dual roles. They have allegiances to their political parties, and the ideologies and expediencies that flow from it. But more importantly, when in public office, they represent public interest. For them to discharge their public duties requires them to exercise forbearance and observe norms of fairness in political life. In a recent book on the American democracy called *How Democracies Die*, Steven Levitsky and Daniel Ziblatt argue that even the most assiduously worded constitutions cannot check the slide into autocracy if they are not underpinned by a set of unwritten norms.[138] They identify these norms as that of mutual toleration—the acceptance of the legitimacy of the political opposition and forbearance, that is the refusal to exercise power to its full legal limits to disable or destroy the Opposition. These norms are not necessarily written into the law, but often exist as political conventions. Therefore, when they are flouted, they do not undermine the legitimacy of public institutions in the same way as flagrant violations of the law does, and escape the same degree of criticism. Yet, they are used by political operators to manipulate the system in their favour, and represent a decaying of the governance systems that sustain the democracy. Democracy can be undermined as easily by ignoring conventions and norms, as they can be by violating laws.

Democratic Backsliding

The term democratic backsliding is often used to describe various kinds of practices that involve the dismantling or compromise of political institutions that sustain a democratic government.

According to political scientist Nancy Bermeo, the classic open-ended coup d'état of the Cold War years are largely in decline. Earlier, a democratic crisis often involved a military coup, where the military or other forces backed by it would illegally oust a democratically elected government. These kinds of coups have marked a large part of the short history of countries like Pakistan. The second kind was an executive coup, which usually involved a democratically elected official suspending the constitutional process to seize power, often in one fell swoop. These were seen in the last fifty years in countries like Philippines, Peru, Armenia and Zambia, but are rarer now. Along with the decrease in open-ended coups and executive coups, there is a general acceptance that with more scrutiny and EVMs, there has also been a marked decrease in election fraud. While electoral malpractice continues in more subtle forms, more flagrant practices such as count falsification, ballot stuffing and ballot-box fraud are much rarer.[139]

Instead, democratic backsliding has taken the new form of executive aggrandizement. Bermeo defines it as the gradual disassembling of institutions that might challenge the executive, in ostensibly legal ways. A notable example of this kind of democratic sliding in recent times is the very large collection of laws passed by President Recep Tayyip Erdoğan in Turkey in the last decade. In Ecuador, Rafael Correa won by a landslide in the past three elections, but also systematically stepped up to compromise several institutions, including the legislature and the opposition parties, and got rid of provisions that limited his term.

There is an ongoing democratic crisis being faced in several established democracies—Poland, Hungary, Turkey, Brazil, South Africa and Israel, to name a few. The gradual dismantling of institutions and mechanisms that check and balance the powers of the executive in liberal democratic constitutional frameworks inevitably leads to a decay of democracy.

There are several institutional checks upon the powers of the executive in a liberal constitutional democratic setup. The most obvious form of accountability is exercised through elections. The threat of losing the next election keeps the executive in check, but for it to have any real bearing, there must be the prerequisite of free and fair elections. Therefore, the executive itself cannot be trusted with the management and the running of elections. There must be independent election management bodies. In India, this role is discharged by the ECI which we will talk about in more detail in the next chapter. While electoral fraud in the form of ballot stuffing and booth capturing has been on the wane, more strategic forms of electoral manipulation have emerged such as using government resources for campaigns, tampering with voter registration, packing electoral commissions and changing electoral policies to favour incumbents. These techniques do not appear fraudulent in the same way as the old methods of fraud, so as not to raise fundamental questions over the fairness of the electoral process.

The Role of Problematic Speech

The unprecedented and rapid rise of extreme speech and misinformation on the media in India is both a cause and a result of democratic backsliding. When political decay reaches advanced stages and the rules of political convention are violated, it leads to loss of public trust in the political process. Such a loss inevitably leads to greater polarization, where the public turns to figures who play on their jingoism and sectarianism, and fuel the already bubbling resentment. This is often marked by unpleasantness in the form of executive hubris, intolerance, distrust, partyism and constrained liberty.

On the other hand, such extreme speech also plays an important role in causing political decay. When speech is polarized, it diverts public attention away from important issues of public interest to zero-sum conflicts about the relative status of different groups in a polity. This causes ruptures in the social fabric of the polity. In India, for instance, the steady increase of religiosity in political life is at the expense of the secular beliefs that have been an intrinsic part of constitutional democracy. More importantly, the existing constitutional framework and the electoral regulations have proven inadequate in addressing the increased use of religion.

Let us take the example of the religious extreme speech in India. Both the Supreme Court and the ECI have been central to the regulation of the use of religion in sectarian politics in India. The conception and parameters of secularism have been established over time by the Supreme Court. Both the Constituent Assembly debates and the Supreme Court's jurisprudence fashion secularism in India towards 'preventing and inhibiting religious and communal conflict and violence'. The state was intended to maintain a distance from religious institutions, while allowing for political or state intervention in religion in order to 'secure a dignified life for all, prevent discrimination on grounds of religion, check religious bigotry, and manage frenzied internecine conflicts that plunge societies into barbarism and into an escalating spiral of violence and cruelty'.

However, both the Supreme Court and the ECI have, in the recent past, failed to curb the amount of religiosity, often used as divisive speech in India's elections. This is despite the existence of stringent laws on the use of religion in elections. The Representation of the People Act of 1951 contains prohibitions on appeals to religion by candidates and political parties in elections. In earlier cases, the court had said that only a candidate's appeals on the basis of their religion, or on the basis of the religion of an opposing candidate, was prohibited. In 2017, the Supreme Court took a harsher view of political speech based on these provisions. The court viewed these prohibitions stringently and also found any reference to religion, caste, race or community of the candidate, the candidate's opponent, or of the voters, in order to secure votes in an election or to discourage voters from voting for a candidate's opponent, as punishable. One would imagine that these legal standards would ensure that religious appeals were not made during elections in India, but that is far from the truth, particularly in recent times.

During the 2017 Gujarat state assembly elections, the electoral battle was framed as one between 'RAM' (the name of the Hindu king and incarnation of the Hindu god Vishnu)—an acronym based on Gujarat Chief Minister Vijay Rupani, BJP President Amit Shah and Prime Minister Narendra Modi—and 'HAJ' (the annual Muslim pilgrimage)—an acronym of opposition leaders Hardik Patel, Alpesh Thakor and Jignesh Mevani. In the 2019 elections, there were several references made to religion by the different parties. Yogi Adityanath, the chief minister of Uttar Pradesh, said the battle between the BJP and other parties was the battle between Bajrangbali and Ali, thus pitching it as a battle between Hindus and Muslims. Adityanath also said that the Opposition parties had been infected by the 'green virus', and that Hindus had no option but to vote for the BJP. The main Opposition party has also rediscovered religious appeal as central to its political strategy. Upon being appointed the Congress president before the Gujarat elections in 2017, Rahul Gandhi kicked off his campaign with a visit to the famous Somnath Temple in Gujarat. He subsequently visited several temples during the Gujarat elections, and continued the practice over the next two years leading up to the 2019 elections.

The Parliament

As we discussed earlier, the Parliament plays one of the most important deliberative functions in a democracy. Increasingly, the Parliament in India seems to be playing that role less and less. Our Parliament meets for a limited number of days, and its sessions are often adjourned for large parts.

No Leader of Opposition

The size of the mandate that the BJP won in 2014 as well as the poor performance of the main Opposition party, the Congress, meant that they won only forty-four seats. Since 1977, the leader of the Opposition is a position recognized by the Speaker of the House. One of the rules of procedure of the Lok Sabha on the recognition of a parliamentary party or group requires that the strength of the party be at least equal to the quorum of the House, which is fifty-five seats. It is worth noting that this rule about recognition of a party and the leader of the Opposition has in fact been rendered redundant by a constitutional amendment, under which even a one-member party is recognized as a legislature party. More importantly, the legislation governing the position of the leader of the Opposition has no such conditions and only requires the leader to be from a party in Opposition to the government having the greatest numerical strength.

Yet the attorney general (another institution which is supposed to be independent) gave a contrary view. The leader of the Opposition is not a mere figurehead. By denying the position, the Speaker also denied resources in the form of salary and secretarial staff. Even more significantly, over time, the leader of the Opposition has come to play a role in the appointment of several members in the other institutions meant to play a balancing role on the executive. The process for these appointments was severely compromised, either through delays or by giving the executive an unchecked role in making them.

The Money Bill Route

Over the last few years, several legalizations have been passed as money bills in the Parliament. The passage of the Aadhaar Act as a money bill in 2016 attracted significant attention, but this is only one of several such cases. Money bills are a category of financial bills that contain provisions related only to taxation, financial obligations of the government, expenditure from or receipt to the public exchequer. Money bills are peculiar in that they can only be introduced in the Lok Sabha where they can be passed by a simple majority. Following this, they are transmitted to the Rajya Sabha. The Rajya Sabha's powers are restricted to giving recommendations on the Bills and sending them back to the Lok Sabha, which the Lok Sabha is under no obligation to accept.

When the ruling party is in minority in the Rajya Sabha, the money bill route has been used to circumvent it several times in the past. However, in recent years, the number of laws mischievously classified as money bills have been unprecedented. These attempts to pass off financial bills like the Aadhaar Bill as money bills erode the supervisory role Rajya Sabha is supposed to play. While the Aadhaar Bill attracted a lot of criticism, this modus operandi has begun to systematically undercut the Rajya Sabha. Other examples include the use of money bills to amend and retrospectively validate campaign contributions, which had been declared illegal by the courts. Electoral bonds were also instituted using the money bill route, to permit unlimited and anonymous corporate donations to political parties.

The Position of the Speaker

From validating several proposed laws as money bills, contrary to the spirit and text of the Constitution, to inexplicably delaying a no-confidence motion against the government, in the past few years, the office of the Speaker has been discharged in a manner that raises serious questions on its independence. On one occasion, the Speaker also imposed a 'guillotine' to prevent any debate and discussion for the passing of the last full Budget (of the sixteenth Lok Sabha). This was widely seen as a way to avoid discussion on issues of financial irregularities and farmer crises.

The Judiciary

Anybody who has followed the decisions, reasonings and positions taken by the Supreme Court in the last few years will be struck by the remarkable institutional dissonance that it suffers from. At various points in the history of the Supreme Court, certain discernible trends can be identified, which seem to influence a large number of decisions. In the first two decades after independence, the court's interpretation was mostly textual, sticking to the Constitution and relying heavily on the Constituent Assembly Debates. In the next phase, the courts were much more willing to move beyond a textual reading, and a more structural and ethical reading of the Constitution was encouraged, and fundamental rights in particular became the norm. In the next phase, there was a drop in judicial discipline as the courts began to sit in smaller benches of two, with decisions becoming much more result-oriented, 'detached from precedent, doctrine and established interpretive methods'. We have entered a fourth phase where judicial incongruence has reached new heights, sometimes even involving the same judges. This institutional dissonance, as I will argue below, is a reflection of the changing nature of democratic practices.

Judicial Inconsistency

Judges appear to pick and choose issues, and what kind of ideological position may drive them on any given day. In a matter of only a few months, we have had the court, and in many instances, the same judges, taking starkly divergent approaches and positions in the matter of law. In August 2017, nine judges of the Supreme Court pronounced one of the most emphatic decisions in the history of Indian jurisprudence protecting fundamental rights. They upheld the right to privacy as a constitutional right, recognizing its broad contours that related not only to physical privacy, but also to various dimensions of bodily integrity, and expectations about information privacy. Most importantly, privacy inheres within the idea of human dignity, which affords all individuals the autonomy of their decisions. This decision was cathartic not only for the petitioners, but also for the public, which had witnessed its privacy trampled upon by both the state and the corporations.

Yet, at the same time, two of the same judges, Justices Dipak Misra and D.Y. Chandrachud, were also involved in hearing a prolonged matter in which a lower court had annulled a marriage between an adult woman, who had converted to Islam, and an adult Muslim man, and directed the woman to be taken into the custody of her parents. This case, which dealt with such a blatant case of interference with a woman's autonomy, should have seen an immediate dismissal of the lower court's judgement. Yet, the same judges who waxed eloquent about decisional autonomy in the privacy case dithered and delayed the matter, ordering a probe by the Central Intelligence Agency to determine the woman's state of mind, and took their own sweet time before arriving at a decision. Even though the court finally did set aside the annulment, the fact that it took several hearings, and did not provide any relief for so long, shows its hesitance to rule in cases where the matter may be controversial. In the privacy case, the coverage in the media and the widespread public opinion were in favour of a finding for privacy. Yet, when they had to apply the same standards for matters that could be more controversial, in this case drawing from the misplaced majoritarian insecurity about love jihad, they were much more evasive.

Judicial Delays

In the Aadhaar matter, the court's dithering knew no bounds. In 2015, the court had passed an order that Aadhaar could be used as an ID only for a limited number of government programmes, which were the Public Distribution System (PDS) scheme, the liquefied petroleum gas (LPG) distribution scheme, the Mahatma Gandhi National Rural Employment Gurantee Act (MGNREGA), the National Social Assistance Programme (Old Age Pensions, Widow Pensions, Disability Pensions), the Prime Minister's Jan Dhan Yojana (PMJDY) and the Employees' Provident Fund Organisation (EPFO). It had emphasized again that enrolling in the Aadhaar scheme was purely voluntary and could not be made mandatory until the matter was decided by the court. Yet, in the next two years, government data shows that Aadhaar authentication was required to avail benefits from 139 welfare schemes (this position has since changed after the final judgement). While the court had already passed its judgements, clearly stating the services for which Aadhaar could be used, in another matter, some judges made stray statements encouraging the use of the Aadhaar number for other services.

The lack of judicial discipline, witnessed in the previous phase of the Supreme Court's history, now not only extended to how precedents were applied in difficult cases but also to basic things such as what matters would be heard, how benches would be allocated cases, delays in providing interim reliefs until too late, and delaying the hearing of important cases. Some of the recent cases that were delayed so long that any possible remedies were severely compromised. These were the Aadhaar case, the dismissal of Alok Verma as the CBI director, the Hadiya case, the constitutionality of electoral bonds and the judicial challenge to demonetization. That is a long list of extremely important cases in a very short period of time. This lack of judicial coherence cannot even be tied clearly to a result-oriented approach seen in the previous phase, where courts were most concerned with the arriving of a ruling they deemed fair, without giving enough consideration to how that ruling was reasoned. The idiosyncrasies of the court in the recent past cannot even be seen as closely tied to its duty of delivering justice. Now judicial decisions seem to draw their direction from some principle of expediency, which is variously driven by popular opinion and political compulsion.

Moral Authority

The court's moral authority is also questioned due to the manner in which the powers of the Office of the Chief Justice have been discharged. Justice Dipak Misra, during his tenure as the chief justice, constituted and headed a bench by himself that quashed investigative proceedings into a bribery scandal that implicated him, creating an exception for the chief justice from conflict-of-interest rules. He also allegedly constituted the bench to hear a petition seeking a review of the vice president's decision to not allow an opposition motion to impeach him to proceed. Some of these developments led to four senior judges of the court calling a press conference to express dissatisfaction about the manner in which the court was being administered. This questionable conduct continued when one of these four judges, Justice Gogoi, succeeded Misra as the chief justice. When accused of sexual harassment by a court employee, he reacted by convening a special bench on the spot himself against all tenets of natural justice, terming it a high-level conspiracy against the judiciary threatening its existence. The attorney general and solicitor general, who are also independent officers of the court and preside over offices meant to ensure accountability, also gathered in the courtroom to character-assassinate the accuser.

Shifting Public Discourse

While these developments in both the judiciary and the legislature are unrelated to the use of social media and technology in the democratic process, one may wonder why I dwell on them here. The nature of misinformation that justifies these events as 'legal' or not overtly fraudulent are, in my opinion, a reflection of how the nature of public discourse, messaging and political strategies have evolved. There are several communication strategies employed to give these constitutional infractions the veneer of legitimacy, which directly relate to the primary subject of this book. As observed by Zeynep Tufekci, a Turkish writer, the networked spaces that we occupy do not necessarily mean only digital spaces. The physical spaces have been reconfigured by the digital spaces, and when we observe social phenomena around networked spaces, it also includes offline and physical spaces that are reconfigured.[140]

In the Aadhaar matter, for instance, the court did not engage in any factual scrutiny of the representations made by the government about the benefits of the project. Several judicial innovations have been evolved by the court over time to deal with questions of fact. In the past, judges have set up commissions for the purpose of carrying out inquiries and reporting to the court. In cases that require expert knowledge to provide an accurate depiction of facts, the court has also appointed committees of experts to provide considered determinations. This suggested a faith in a considered process where issues of fact needed to be borne out clearly. In recent times, the court has been relying almost entirely on affidavits from public servants, and does not see within its role the need to question the assertions in them, even as they are being fact-checked in the media. Even when detailed investigative reports were presented before the court, it refused to engage with them on the grounds that it had no tools at its disposal to test their veracity.[141] This tenuous relationship with the sanctity of truth is a sign of the times. When legitimate news reports are painted with the same brush as organized misinformation, any report can be painted as 'biased', 'politically motivated' or 'fake'.

The volume of extreme speech and misinformation outside of these institutional discussions also creates ripe opportunities for them to be co-opted within the institutional discourse. During discussions on money bills, the leaders of both the Houses of Parliament, Prime Minister Modi in the Lok Sabha and Finance Minister Arun Jaitely in the Rajya Sabha, have pointed to previous examples of money bills such as the Juvenile Justice Bill of 1986 and the African Development Bill of 1989. Congress leader Jairam Ramesh was so shocked at this constitutional impropriety that he took it upon himself to look up the history of the past bills in the Parliament library. The minister found that the past bills were not money bills at all, and the assertions of the leaders of both the Houses were false.[142] In this case, it appeared that Finance Minister Jaitely may have been misled by a factual error on the Lok Sabha's website. However, such errors are reflective of the tendency to rewrite history in the manner that suits one's agenda.

The courts, as well as the legislature, have, in their own ways, both contributed to the decay in the premium placed on the value of truth in public discourse, as well as fallen victim to it. By allowing parties to get away with anything less than the objective truth, they have played their part in reducing its value in public discourse, and also adding legitimacy to the versions of facts that have gone uncontested. The loss of an accepted core of objective facts inevitably leads to polarized politics and sectarianism, as has happened in India.

CHAPTER 9

The Election Commission's Crisis of Credibility

The Election Commission is one of the most trusted public institutions in India. This is supported by survey data and studies from a range of disciplines over the last two decades. The vibrant Indian electorate has, on the whole, accepted electoral outcomes, which has made the peaceful transition of power from one elected government to another possible for almost seven decades.

—Ornit Shani, author and political scholar

The ECI administered the 17th general election, where 65 per cent of over 800 million eligible voters cast their ballots—a mammoth and admirable task any day.[143] More than 10 million polling officials and security personnel staffed around 9,30,000 polling stations.[144] Results were announced as per schedule on 23 May 2019. Elections in India are a fairly complex process. Keeping in mind the Herculean task of organizing and managing fair elections across the country at all levels, the Constitution of India, under Article 324(1), has vested in the ECI the superintendence, direction and control of the entire process for conducting elections to Parliament and the legislature of every state, and to the offices of the president and the vice president of India. If elections are the most fundamental feature of a democracy, the ECI plays the single most important role in furthering and preserving that democracy in India. As stated earlier, after independence, nearly 200 million uneducated and unpropertied Indians were provided franchise—there were serious doubts about the capacity of the Indian state to conduct free and fair elections.[145]

In the previous chapter, we have discussed in detail how the health of a democratic setup is directly dependent on the independence and robustness of its institutions. In order to effectively exercise checks and balances on an elected government, the public institutions such as the election management bodies must enjoy the trust of the people. The ECI has accumulated trust over decades of successfully conducted elections. Various problems that threaten the very basis of the legitimacy of an elected government—such as poor turnout of voters, booth capturing, political patronage through buying of votes in lieu of cash, jobs and other benefits, and problematic behaviour of political parties during elections—have regularly challenged the ECI. But the ECI has incrementally worked to continue to build and preserve trust in the electoral process in India.

During the first elections, over 80 per cent of the electorate was illiterate, and a similar number had very little or no property to speak of.[146] Contrary to what we may imagine now, the decision to provide franchise to all adult citizens was not an obvious one. In the US, the women were granted the right to vote only in 1920, over 130 years after its first elections. The UK granted an extended franchise to women in 1932, also a century after its first elections. France and Italy had only recently followed suit. At the time of independence, Australia did not allow its aborigines to vote, nor did Switzerland allow its women to. But 1952 onwards, even the most oppressed of India's population were eligible to vote. In fact, Article 324 of the Constitution, from which the ECI derives its legitimacy, was enforced, along with the very first provisions, on 26 November 1949, a good two months before India became a republic—and a day before that, on 25 January 1950, the ECI was created.

A Democracy's Habit of Mind

Over seventeen general elections, and scores of other elections, electoral outcomes have become the default in India, and there is no question of having any alternative to the peaceful transition of power from one elected body to the next. In the 1950s, this was not a given, nor did many expect it. The trust in the electoral system that India enjoys over many other countries that became independent around the same time is largely owed to the ECI's efforts, starting from the very first elections in 1952. The ECI then had the unenviable task of preparing the electoral rolls for the first elections. The Partition led to the displacement of over 15 million people, and about 85 per cent of the first electorate in India in 1952 had never voted before. The task of preparing for the first elections had begun even before the creation of the ECI, in September 1947, by a small body, which was part of the Constituent Assembly, called the Constituent Assembly Secretariat (CAS). Ornit Shani, the author of *How India Became Democratic: Citizenship and the Making of the Universal Franchise*, argues that the responsive manner in which the CAS, 'as the election management body at the time, dealt with the registration of voters, and particularly with the many challenges that arose in that process, cultivated the engagement and trust of the future electorate'.[147]

The handling of the citizens' contestations over a place on the roll by the CAS is all the more instructional, given the recent controversies over the removal of names from electoral rolls in states like Andhra Pradesh as a result of technological attempts to remove frauds or bogus names from the rolls. The CAS's adoption of practices and norms of openness and responsiveness is in stark contrast to the opacity and general high-handedness with which names are removed from the rolls using Aadhaar-based authentication, or the draconian regulation to weed out illegal immigrants under the National Register of Citizens in Assam. Shani describes how the initial rules 'for the preparation of the rolls set out that a voter had to be a citizen of or above twenty-one years of age, with a place of residence in the electoral unit where he or she was to be registered for a period of no less than 180 days in the year ending on 31 March 1948, i.e. no later than 30 September 1947'. It was, however, quickly realized that these rules were unworkable and would result in the omission of names from the rolls of most of the refugees from Pakistan and Bangladesh. The CAS first tried to look at past experiences with refugees in other countries and prepared a report on international precedents. When none of the collected approaches seemed appropriate, the CAS observed that 'the refugees are always on the move, and therefore, no residential qualification can be prescribed for them, if they are to be given the right of vote in the next elections'.[148] It was finally decided that the refugees would be permitted to be enrolled on the mere declaration by them of their intention to reside permanently in the town or village concerned, irrespective of the actual period of residence.

Despite this express instruction, many people were faced with varying kinds of exclusionary practices followed by the provincial governments and local officials. These challenges were not unexpected in a polity that lacked strong local institutions and adequate means of representation. However, the CAS, despite being a centralized body, painstakingly responded to these challenges—responding to all complaints and requests for clarifications within two weeks, and summoning local officials with exclusionary practices such as the imposition of a court fee to make the declaration of intent to reside. It even resorted to making specific inquiries into complaints and reports of misconduct and negligence, and taking steps to publicize comprehensive information on problems that arose with faulty procedures and the manner in which they were redressed. These, and many other steps, by the CAS and the ECI in its early days—aptly described by Dr S. Radhakrishnan as the electoral democracy's 'habit of mind... its spirit, that sensitive adjustment...to the infinitely varied demands of other persons'—went a long way in building trust in the electoral process in India from the beginning.[149]

A Study in Contrast

Contrast this with the deletion of roughly 10 per cent of the electorate from the rolls during the state assembly elections in Telangana in 2015 during the process of removing frauds and duplicates from the electoral rolls. During the state assembly elections in 2018, it emerged that over 30 lakhs voters could have been disenfranchized.[150] There have been similar reports of 'cleaning up' exercises from states such as Andhra Pradesh, Uttarakhand and Rajasthan. In 2019, Srinivas Kodali, a security researcher, filed a petition in the Hyderabad High Court challenging the constitutionality of such cleaning-up exercises, as well as seeking details about the process followed for it. It appears that in the case of Telangana, the deletions were a result of the seeding of Aadhaar numbers with Voter ID numbers.[151]

While the need to remove duplicates from electoral rolls is a legitimate one, the use of automated technology to do so, without any provision for recourse to corrective measures by those unjustly impacted, sets a dangerous precedent. In this case, there is blind reliance on the robustness of an 'infallible' technology, without accounting for the real-life experiences of people and the many ways it prejudices those who are unjustly removed.

Hyderabad was a pilot project for Aadhaar and EPIC (Electoral Photo Identity Card) card seeding. The process of seeding essentially involved algorithmically using Aadhaar numbers and related demographic information to search for corresponding entries in other databases such as, in this case, the electoral roll's database. Srinivas Kodali, an independent researcher working on data and the Internet, said that he suspected that if there were any differences in demographic data between the EPIC database and Aadhaar database, they might be used to delete the entries from the EPIC databases. This was an exercise carried out by the State Election Commission and not the UIDAI, the parent body that administers the Aadhaar programme in India. The State Election Commission sought the use of a facility called DSDV (Destination Sequenced Distance Vector) routing from the UIDAI. This tool would allow them to carry out the 'purification' of electoral databases by comparing them against the Aadhaar demographic data.[152]

This exercise was based on the assumption that the Aadhaar database, due to its robust process of duplication using fingerprint authentication, was the most accurate and reliable one. Very early, in the days after the inception of the Aadhaar project, it was assumed that this database would serve as the authoritative determinant of identification, and over time, would be used to rid other databases of duplicates. Other databases often have ghosts and duplicates, as well as suffer from poor practices of data collection. However, this process of deletion of entries from other databases assumes that all entries that do not match with the Aadhaar data are false and mala fide. This is clearly not the case.

Often government databases suffer from poor data collection practices. It is not uncommon for the EPIC database to have incorrectly spelt demographic details such as name, address and father's name. My own name is spelt incorrectly on my EPIC card, but I was permitted to vote in the seventeenth general elections after the voting officer verified my identity against my photograph and other demographic details. To attribute mala fide intent to all mistakes in such databases and to summarily delete them is grossly negligent, and goes a long way in damaging the hard-earned trust in the electoral process in India.

Aside from automated deletion, the process of deletion of voters from the electoral rolls is also prone to errors, and from all accounts, very easy to manipulate. In the case of Andhra Pradesh, the ongoing investigations have reportedly revealed that TDP party workers would use the Seva Mitra app to profile voters, and determine how likely they were to support the party.[153] In order to do this, they would apparently use automated voice calling services to reach out to potential voters, and based on their response, assign them a score on their likelihood of voting for the party. Once they had compiled a list of those who had a low score, and consequently, in their estimation, were unlikely to vote for the party, they would file a Form 7 objection against them. Form 7 is a feature provided by the ECI. Anyone can file this form to object to a name on the electoral rolls. Once filed, the ECI is supposed to physically verify whether the person has shifted base, or is deceased, or is a duplicate, and if that is the case, remove the name.[154] It is unclear how rigorously these steps are being followed as several reports of people finding their names on the voters' list have emerged.

The Model Code of Conduct

Prior to the elections, the ECI announces the MCC, which is a set of instructions to be followed during election campaigning. The MCC lacks legislative authority and is a non-binding set of guidelines issued by the ECI that regulates the conduct of political parties and candidates in the immediate run-up to the elections. It comes into force from the time the ECI announces the election dates. In current times—where politicians are constantly in campaign mode—this illusory idea that the election campaign only begins once the dates for an election have been announced has no basis in reality. Very little is achieved by limiting the code of conduct to a time period, which is barely a month before elections begin. Moreover, in the case of the 17th Lok Sabha elections, the dates were, in fact, even less than a month apart.

The idea of the MCC, which began with state elections in Kerala in 1960, has incrementally grown over time. To begin with, the MCC only regulated election meetings, speeches and slogans. From

1979 onwards, the MCC started paying special attention to the political party in power and included recommendations to prevent it from using the state machinery to its advantage. For instance, it prohibits appointed ministers from combining official visits with election campaigns, using official machinery, personnel and government vehicles for electioneering, and using government platforms for political advertising. Over time, the MCC has come to include guidelines on general conduct, meetings, procession, polling day, polling booth, observers and election manifestos.

The MCC is often blamed as a toothless document, as its violation by itself does not result in any penalties from the ECI, aside from reprimands. The only legal recourse is to file a criminal complaint before a court of law. In case of violations of the MCC, the ECI can issue a notice to the candidate or the political party for breach. The party served with the notice is required to respond in writing. The ECI's power is essentially limited to a written censure of the offending act. In extreme cases, the ECI can file a criminal complaint against the offending party. However, as S.Y. Quraishi, former chief election commissioner, puts it, an active ECI can make a huge difference, and even a note of caution made publicly to parties carries a great deal of weight.[155] Even though the MCC does not have legal backing, the ECI has several options at its disposal, from naming and shaming to imposing restrictions on campaigning activities of defaulting parties, and, in extreme cases, even changing the dates of elections.

Political Conduct on Social Media

The MCC only regulates the conduct of political parties and candidates, but not that of other stakeholders who may be involved in the electoral process. The ECI invited several Internet companies, including Google, Facebook and ShareChat, to participate in the creation of a Voluntary Code of Ethics for the General Elections, in March 2019. Recognizing the increasing impact that the use of social media was having on electoral processes, the stated purpose of the code was 'to identify measures [...] put in place to increase confidence in the electoral process'. The companies engaged in this process under the leadership of the Internet and Mobile Association of India (IMAI) presented the Code to the ECI on 20 March 2019.[156]

The focus of this code was to have greater transparency in paid political advertising. It essentially brought political advertisements on social media platforms such as Facebook and Twitter under the MCC. In the same manner, as has been the case with newspaper and radio advertisements, parties were now required to disclose expenditure accounts for social media advertisement. This was done by allowing advertisers to submit pre-certificates issued by the ECI and the Media Certification and Monitoring Committee (MCMC) in relation to election advertisements that featured names of political parties or candidates for the upcoming elections. The candidates were also required to submit details of their social media accounts at the time of filing nominations. Other commitments included having direct channels of communication between the companies and the ECI to facilitate speedy resolution of any complaints. Candidates and parties had to declare expenditure on social media, making it part of the overall spending limit.

Neither the ECI nor the Representation of Peoples Act specifies a definition of the term 'political advertising'. Largely, the various Internet platforms were left to individually determine how they would govern political advertising. Google, for instance, includes four kinds of users whose advertising would fall under the purview of political advertising. It would include (1) political parties (2) businesses (3) non-profit organizations and (4) individuals, and the criteria for classifying an advertisement as political was that it must feature a political party.[157]

On the other hand, Twitter defined three categories of political advertising: (1) Ads purchased by a political party (2) Ads purchased by a candidate and (3) Ads advocating for a clearly identified candidate or political party. Although the MCC guidelines in 2019 require that all political parties and candidates do disclose their expenditure on social media advertisements, there is no attempt to regulate the expenditure on advertising by the diffusely connected supporters who do not directly contribute to party funding but may support the candidates through coordinated advertising. In some cases, the platforms have attempted to introduce some accountability in this unregulated space. Key examples of measures include a requirement on paid advertising to carry disclaimers, take down procedures when this is not followed, and a public repository to easily access such advertisements and expenditures.

The Regulatory Vacuum of Diffuse Actors

While these measures by the Internet platforms go above and beyond what the ECI expects of them, they remain fairly inadequate. Even these measures get only partly implemented. The legal recourse under the Indian Penal Code (IPC) for ghost advertising is Section 171. It penalizes election advertising on behalf of candidates without their authorization, but only specifies a fine of ₹500. Compare this paltry fine with the amount of money spent on platform advertising. Nidhi Singh and Gunjan Chawla of the Centre for Communication Governance, National Law University Delhi, reported that the expenditure of the top ten Facebook pages for political advertisement for the months of February and March in 2019 amounted to ₹61,324,689. Singh and Chawla found that out of these ten pages, one was registered under the BJP's name, one under the Biju Janata Dal's name, but the remaining eight were all registered under the names of private parties with no clear political affiliations. Even more importantly, despite Facebook's policies, four of them did not even have disclaimers that they were political advertisements.[158]

This is highly problematic, with the emergence of diffuse and amorphous machinery, which is involved in the creation and dissemination of extreme speech online. Aside from candidates, political party cadres and karyakartas, there is now a team of floating groups of volunteers that is only indirectly connected to a campaign, but plays the role of active vote mobilizers. The role of these vote mobilizers in the 2014 elections seems to have been significant. While the landslide victories in the 2014 and 2019 elections are attributed almost singly to the role of Narendra Modi as a star campaigner, most of the literature on leadership effects says that the presence of a leader should not be a large factor in the elections. Leadership effects become more significant where there is the absence of a strong, institutionalized and ideological party that has a partisan base. These are all factors that do not hold true for the BJP. It is, in fact, among all Indian political parties, the one that is an institutionalized party with an ideological leaning and a partisan base. Even more importantly, the BJP is closely aligned with a well-organized social group—the Rashtriya Swayamsevak Sangh (RSS). Political parties that are closely associated with social organizations are less leader-centric, and more cadre-centric.

Let us take a look at the impact Narendra Modi had as a prime ministerial candidate. If we look closely at the 2014 elections, there was a marked change in public opinion in support of the BJP between 2013 and 2014. In June 2013, the data from National Election Studies conducted by the Lokniti programme of the Centre for the Study of Developing Societies (CSDS), before and after each Lok Sabha election, showed that 27 per cent of the people who polled had planned to vote for the BJP, while another 27 per cent had planned to vote for the Congress.[159] Just a year later, the post-poll data from the National Election Studies showed that 36 per cent of the respondents said they preferred Modi as prime minister, as compared to the 19 per cent who had said so in 2013. This would run counter to the argument made in the previous paragraph about the impact of a leader on the fortunes of an institutionally robust party like the BJP. However, as political scientists Pradeep Chhibber and Susan Ostermann point out, we may be looking at the wrong parameter to judge the impact of a candidate like Modi.

Research shows that as opposed to the direct leadership effect of Narendra Modi on the BJP, it was his ability to attract vote mobilizers in large numbers that won him and the BJP such support. Vote mobilizers are traditionally individuals whose support for a particular party goes beyond simple voting, and instead, involves monetary donations, door-to-door canvassing and leaflet/poster distribution. In recent times, and in both the 2014 and the 2019 elections, the significant role of vote mobilizers has been in stirring up support on social media. Analysis done by Chhibber and Ostermann on the National Election Studies data showed that only a small proportion of BJP's vote mobilizers were party members. The rest had no institutional affiliation to the party and not part of any regulatory structures.

In his book *War Room: The People, Tactics and Technology behind Narendra Modi's 2014 Win*, N.P. Ullekh highlights the role played by Prashant Kishor's NGO CAG—in the general elections. Kishor, who had been part of Modi's team during the 2012 state assembly elections in Gujarat, realized the need to have a team to run a presidential-style campaign. CAG recruited graduates from the Indian Institutes of Management (IIMs), the Indian Institutes of Technology (IITs), the Indian School of Business (ISB), Stanford, Cornell, national law schools and those who had worked in the finance and marketing teams at JP Morgan, Michelin India, International Business Machines Corporation (IBM), Barclays Capital, Merrill Lynch, Deutsche Bank, McKinsey & Company and Goldman Sachs. CAG went about youth mobilization systematically. In September 2013, they organized a large event called 'Manthan'. The supposed aim of this conference was to involve the youth in shaping the agenda of the next elections, and connecting them with policymakers. They had online forums with a list of fourteen questions for which they sought solutions and ideas. They got 20,000 responses from 700 colleges. The next step was to have 500 'campus ambassadors' visit college campuses, select the best responses and arrange for them to meet with leaders in power. CAG was able to involve about 5 lakh youth in this process. It was through this process that they began building a diffuse team of educated, young people across the country to help with the campaign.

In each parliamentary constituency, there were one or two CAG members working closely with RSS-BJP leaders, and they were assisted by many more volunteers who kept enrolling from these regions. Ullekh reports that CAG created 316 Facebook pages for various Lok Sabha constituencies, out of which 160 were given primacy based on research that they were identified as higher impact constituencies for digital reach. These Facebook pages set up were soon inundated with requests for direct interaction with Narendra Modi, which led to the famous 'Chai Pe Charcha', a regular video-conferencing initiative in which Modi would host events from tea stalls in Ahmedabad, which would be relayed across 1,000 more tea stalls in 300 cities. This served the twin purpose of both co-opting the 'chaiwala' tag that the Opposition had used misguidedly against him, as well as underline the insight that tea in India serves as a social binder and acts as a setup for both formal and informal discussions. Implementing this concept was a mammoth task, which again the CAG and its network of volunteers played a key role in. Modi would address people gathered at tea stalls at 1,500 select locations and later answer their questions and listen to their grievances. The proceedings of the programme were to be instantly translated into local languages in non-Hindi-speaking states. To begin with, CAG single-handedly identified and set up 'Chai Pe Charcha' tea stalls with assistance from its volunteer base—lakhs of whom had approached them through local BJP party offices or through online and offline media.[160]

Communications scholar Sahana Udupa has written on vote mobilizers, drawing on her research involving ethnographic fieldwork among politically active online users in Mumbai, Delhi and Bengaluru, which started in 2013, and social media content and network analysis of online exchange based on purposive sampling. According to her, one of the categories was 'techie-turned-ideologue', which primarily involved technically trained, English-speaking and social-media-adept volunteers. They did not take any money from the party and did the work out of 'passion'. Then there were monetized actors who built online pages, often appealing to Hindutva actors, but now also those who attack Hindu nationalism. The primary motivation for these actors is to make money by building an online following, which could later be monetized with advertisements. Then there were actors whose ideology and business interests combined. Udupa gave the example of an ardent Modi supporter whose 'digital influence work for a local BJP leader started because of sheer compulsion of gaining the first contract for his just-launched digital media company'. Often it leads to not just direct business opportunities, but also opportunities to access powerful people in the party and government.[161] At this point, there are no existing forms of regulations that address this kind of diffuse behaviour, and neither is the law nor the ECI in a position to regulate the funding of such actors.

PART FIVE
Public Forums of Internet Platforms

CHAPTER 10
Regulating Internet Intermediaries

Tech firms are already transferring their economic power into political power through lobbying, but they differ from 'traditional' monopolies in important ways: by owning the platforms on which material is published, they have an important influence over public opinion and activism itself. This has important ramifications for how citizens practise 'free association', which is the basis of all independent civil society and a bulwark against tyranny.

—Jamie Bartlett, author and journalist

The last few years have seen ongoing public relations nightmares for large technological platform companies. In the US, large companies such as Facebook, Google and Twitter have had to endure rigorous questioning from the government, including a congressional testimony to explain the role their platforms may have played in a covert Russian operation to manipulate the US elections. In India, too, tech giants have come under significant attention since 2018.

On 26 July 2018, Ravi Shankar Prasad, the IT Minister of India, was giving a speech in the Rajya Sabha, the Upper House of the Parliament. He warned that social media platforms could not 'evade their responsibility, accountability and larger commitment to ensure that their platforms were not misused on a large scale to spread incorrect facts projected as news and designed to instigate people to commit crime'. More ominously, he said that if 'they do not take adequate and prompt action, then the law of abetment also applies to them'. The minister was speaking in response to the rising incidents of mob lynchings in India, ostensibly occasioned by the spreading of misinformation, inciting violence on social media and mobile messaging services. Comparing social media services to newspapers, Prasad further said that when there is provocative writing in newspapers, the newspaper could not say that it was not responsible.[162]

Prasad's words of warnings were not in isolation. Since the revelation about Cambridge Analytica's use of Facebook to profile and manipulate users with political content emerged, the Indian government has been engaged in a series of ad hoc communications with large Internet intermediaries.

When the Cambridge Analytica-Facebook data incident was widely reported, the Ministry for Electronics and IT sought details from both Cambridge Analytica and Facebook about how many Indian residents' data was impacted during the incident. While Cambridge Analytica did not provide a clear response, Facebook admitted that the data of 5,60,000 Indians had been compromised. The CBI was tasked with probing possible violations of the Information Technology Act (IT Act), 2000, and the IPC in July. While a threatening message was sent by the ministry, the actual capacity of the government to take any legal action against Facebook or Cambridge Analytica remains legally ambiguous, given the minimal data protection regulation that exists in India.[163]

This data scandal has also been pivotal to the debate on data protection regulations in India and may have directly led to proposals such as data localization—the government wants all online data owned by Indians to remain within the territorial boundaries of India and within Indian jurisdiction.

In 2018, the ministry also engaged in a long, publicly exchanged dialogue with WhatsApp over the issue of the spread of misinformation on the platform that may have played some role in a series of lynchings across the country. The IT ministry sent notices to WhatsApp, insisting, among other demands, that they build traceability of messages on the platforms, and warning that they would be liable to be treated as 'abettors' for crimes committed using the platform. WhatsApp has consistently insisted that this would compromise the end-to-end encryption that users enjoy.[164] Yet again, the threats from the ministry to stop services were on a questionable legal footing.

A study by the Indraprastha Institute of Information Technology, Delhi (IIIT Delhi), analysed 925 names, including those of all the main political parties and key political figures.[165] Among other things, they also analysed the rise and fall in the Twitter following of these names and traced the fall in count followed by a crackdown on fake accounts by Twitter in November 2018. This led to allegations of political bias and members of the Youth for Social Media Democracy organization protesting outside Twitter's office against its 'anti-right-wing attitude'.[166] Soon, the powers that be also took notice. India's parliamentary committee on IT, led by Anurag Thakur, sent a summons to

Twitter representatives to provide testimony on the issue of safeguarding citizens' rights online.

Safe Harbour for Internet Platforms

Questions arise because Internet intermediaries such as Facebook, Twitter and WhatsApp enjoy a safe harbour, which means that they are not responsible for activities conducted by users on their platforms. Most states have chosen to regulate these platforms similarly, by granting them immunity for third-party content. This legal framework, called Intermediary Liability, is responsible for the rapid rise of online platform businesses over the last two decades where platforms can expand their services without having to worry about the legality of the user-generated content on them.

This safe harbour is applied uniformly in most jurisdictions, including India, to a host of intermediaries, including Internet service providers such as Airtel, search engines like Google and Bing, web-hosting providers like Amazon Web Services and Rackspace, e-commerce websites such as Flipkart and Myntra, blogging platforms like WordPress and Tumblr, social media companies such as Facebook, Twitter and Instagram, video-sharing sites such as YouTube, and messaging apps like WhatsApp and WeChat.

This allows intermediaries to not worry about pre-screening all the content that is uploaded on their platforms. Given the sheer scale of information that is transmitted through the Internet, this legal arrangement is perhaps necessary, as most platforms lack the wherewithal to monitor content.

In that respect, it was reasoned that Internet platforms were different from traditional content-dissemination businesses such as newspapers and magazines, even in their online avatars, as they, by their very nature, exercise editorial control over what passes through their platforms. Therefore, while a news website such as The Wire plays an active role in the creation of the content that it publishes, the same cannot be said of news aggregator platforms such as Google News or Dailyhunt, as they merely bring together the various sources of news in one place, but do not play a role in the creation of that content. Similarly, Twitter is primarily in the business of providing a platform for users to express themselves in a limited number of characters, aided with images, GIFs and videos, and allowing engagement through replies, retweets and hashtags—but it does not play any real role in deciding what content is produced.

The form of intermediary liability has also gone through a few different iterations in its short history in India. In 2000, when the IT Act was passed, the first version of this arrangement came into existence. This law provided protection to intermediaries for third-party content as long as they had no knowledge of its illegality or exercised some due diligence. The law first came under scrutiny when, in 2004, a CD of two teenagers engaging in a sexual act was made available for sale on a website called Bazee.com. The item was first listed on the evening of 27 November 2004 on Bazee.com's website and deactivated two days later, on 29 November 2004, after a complaint was lodged. In the meantime, a few sales took place through the website. This case, also likely the first prominent online case of revenge porn, much before the term became popular, led to Avinash Bajaj, the CEO of Bazee.com, being arrested and having to spend a few days in Tihar Jail. Bazee.com was acquired by the Internet giant eBay in a much-publicized $50 million deal. Additionally, as Bajaj was a US citizen, his arrest led to an international incident, with the US secretary of state becoming personally involved in negotiations with the Indian government.[167]

More significantly, perhaps, the case led to calls from the industry for a need to clarify the nature and extent of protection under the safe harbour law. In 2008, the legislation was amended, and a more detailed set of rules on safe harbour was introduced. Now, intermediaries were required to inform users that they were not supposed to post any harmful or illegal content on their websites. The new key development, however, was the introduction of a notice and takedown mechanism. As long as intermediaries took down an illegal piece of content from their platforms within thirty-six hours of being notified about it, they were exempt from liability. This, however, led to several situations where offended parties would reach out to an intermediary about content that they complained was illegal. However, the intermediary, in many cases, was not equipped to decide whether it was indeed illegal. Even in cases where they may have believed that the content was not illegal, they would take it down to avoid the risk of losing their safe harbour protection. Needless to say, this kind of framework was extremely harmful to free speech, as platforms could be held hostage by any offended party and acts of private censorship.

In 2012, the Centre for Internet and Society conducted a study where it sent intentionally flawed takedown notices to a sample comprising seven prominent intermediaries, and documented their responses to the notices. The study looked at different policy factors in the takedown notices to understand at what points in the process of takedown, free expression was being curbed. Of the seven intermediaries to which takedown notices were sent, six intermediaries over-complied with the notices, despite the apparent flaws in them. The study concluded that most of the intermediaries did not have sufficient legal competence or resources to deliberate on the legality of an expression. Even in cases where they had the capacity, it appeared that intermediaries had a tendency to prioritize the allocation of its legal resources according to the commercial importance of impugned expressions. Finally, if such a subjective determination is required to be done in a limited time frame of thirty-six hours and in the absence of adequate facts and circumstances, the intermediary mechanically (without application of mind or proper judgement) will, more often than not, comply with the takedown notice.[168]

In 2012, Shiv Sena leader Bal Thackrey died, and transportation and several services in Mumbai were shut down in preparation of his funeral. A teenage girl posted a statement on Facebook criticizing the city's decision. This led to a complaint filed against her under the IT Act, and the Mumbai police arrested the girl, as well as her friend, who had 'liked' her post on Facebook. This case, which is widely criticized in the media, drew the attention of a twenty-one-year-old law student, Shreya Singhal. Singhal filed a public interest litigation before the Supreme Court, asking for the repeal of the provision under the IT Act, which, among other things, made it a criminal offence to send 'annoying' messages to another person. The language of the law was so vague that it curbed free speech and led to unwanted censorship. The People's Union for Civil Liberties, one of India's oldest and largest civil liberty organizations, was already working on a petition that not only challenged this provision but also the intermediary liability regime. They joined arguments and filed their petition with Singhal. Other petitioners also began to file cases challenging other laws, including the constitutionality of a provision of the Kerala Police

Act, which had similarly been used by law enforcement to arrest speakers for online speech considered 'annoying' or 'indecent'.

Seven lawyers led oral arguments in court, with a team of about fifteen counsels actively supporting them. There were also inputs collected from multiple research institutions and academics. One news report cited that altogether, over ninety attorneys contributed to the petitions, hearings and arguments before the court.[169]

Three years later, in 2015, the Supreme Court read down the provisions of the IT Act. While the offending provisions which criminalized offensive or annoying speech were repealed, they also amended the intermediary liability regime. The court held that Section 79—which allowed the government to hold intermediaries accountable if they had actual knowledge of an infringement—was constitutional. However, the court clearly spelt out what 'actual knowledge' would mean in this case. For the intermediary to have knowledge, there must be a judicial order for removal of content. This meant that rather than leaving it to the esteemed wisdom of the intermediary to determine the illegality of third-party content on their websites, it now required a judicial adjudication.

Once again, Minister Prasad's reliance on the word abetment suggests that the government was re-evaluating the nature of safe harbour. One of the exceptions to the safe harbour says that it will be disqualified if the intermediary has conspired, abetted, aided or induced, whether by threats, promises or otherwise, in the commission of the unlawful act. Late in December 2018, the IT ministry came out with a set of proposed amendments to the intermediary liability law, which undid most of the hard-earned protections to free speech that the Shreya Singhal case had won, and again moved the focus back to the intermediaries to regulate what the draft perceived as 'illegal content'. Among other things, the rules required that the intermediaries proactively monitor and automatically delete 'unlawful content'. This was in direct conflict with the order in the Shreya Singhal case, that intermediaries should only be legally compelled to take down content on the basis of court orders or legally empowered government agencies. On the date of writing this book, the draft rules had not yet been finalized.

Beyond Safe Harbour

One of the key problems with the intermediary liability regime is that it paints all intermediaries with the same brush. As mentioned earlier, the term applies equally to Internet service providers, social media platforms, search engines, private messaging services, e-commerce companies and web-hosting services. The new proposed rules do not disturb this status quo. The basis for safe harbour is the idea that intermediaries are mere dumb conduits for the distribution of the speech of its users, rather than speakers themselves. However, this argument of the dumb conduit is no longer tenable. Most, if not all, intermediaries affirmatively shape the form and substance of user content in some manner, using highly intelligent prioritization algorithms.

First, let us consider the more superficial design features of intermediaries. Take, for instance, Twitter. When Twitter claims safe harbour, it positions itself primarily as a distributor of the users' tweets. However, its user interface is deterministic and affects the nature and content of the tweets. The 140-character limitation (now 280) has led to the evolution of Twitter's own syntax and vocabulary. Subtweets, likes, retweets and hashtags are some of the design features that shape how content is created on such a platform. While these do impact the generation of content, perhaps they are not a sufficient argument against the safe harbour. These features do not render Twitter much more than a thoroughfare for ideas, albeit one with distinct rules on what form those ideas may take.

The more insidious design features, which are more obscure or opaque in nature, are worth looking at more closely. Many intermediaries employ design features to hold our attention by making their interfaces more addictive. Facebook employs techniques to ensure that each user sees stories and updates in their 'News Feed' that they may not have seen on their last visit to the site. It analyses, sorts and reuses user data to make meaning out of their users' 'reactions', search terms and browsing activity in order to curate the content of each user's individual feed, personalized advertisements and recommendations. All of this is done in the garb of improving user experience. Make no mistake, this improvement of user experience is a necessity. Given the deluge of information that exists online, it is indeed desirable that platforms personalize our experience in some manner. But the constant tinkering with user data and targeting of content goes far beyond these necessities.

Essentially, the discovery of information is being transformed from an individual to a social and algorithmic endeavour. On a platform like Facebook, a large portion of users are exposed to news shared by their friends. Selective exposure to opinions of like-minded people is a phenomenon that existed in the pre-digital era as well; however, the ease with which we can find, follow and focus on such people and exclude others in the online world enhances this tendency. The study by Eytan Bakshy and others that we also referred to in Chapter 2 shows that on Facebook, the three filters—the social network, the feed population algorithm and the user's own content selection—combine to decrease exposure to ideologically challenging news from a random baseline by more than 25 per cent for conservative users, and close to 50 per cent for liberal users in the US.[170] However, these statistics are of limited value. The digression of 25 per cent to 50 per cent assumes that the baseline is a completely bias-free exposure, which is never the case. In fact, there is now evidence to suggest that those who are only on mainstream media may suffer from being in an ideological bubble even more so. While we remain unsure of the exact impact social media platforms have on ideological leanings, it does seem clear that they intermediate our access to information in ways that shape our engagement significantly. There is little empirical work on the subject in India, but it is clear that exposure to diverse views suffers on a platform like Facebook for Indian users as well.

There is a definite need for differentiating between infrastructure information intermediaries (such as ISPs) and content information intermediaries that facilitate communication (such as social media networks). It might be possible to create content-neutral standards for infrastructure information intermediaries that do not primarily focus on content transmission. For example, a set of content-neutral standards (like common carrier regulations) could apply to infrastructure intermediaries, while separate standards that are not content-neutral would apply to content intermediaries. Given the full and total control over our user experience online, intermediaries do owe us a duty of care. The right to free speech and protection of equality and dignity are recognized by most constitutions around the world, and consequently, have to be preserved by the state in its attempts to regulate public discourse. However, in the absence of a comparable obligation on online platforms, they are free to permit and ban any categories of speech, notwithstanding the monumental role they play in navigating global discourse.

CHAPTER 11
Platforms as Public Spheres

Such use of the...public places has, from ancient times, been a part of the privileges, immunities, rights and liberties of citizens.

—Hague vs. Committee for Industrial Organization

The narrative that big tech is an existential threat to democracy is somewhere between an emerging concern and a state of moral panic. It is, however, clear that the large platforms enjoy considerable power to shape and steer public discourse. Zuckerberg once notoriously remarked that Facebook had grown more like a government than a traditional company.[171] If one were to stretch that analogy, one-fourth of the world's population and a similar proportion of India's population is now subject to the laws of Facebook's terms and conditions, and privacy policies. There are now over 260 million monthly users on YouTube.[172] Twitter, despite having a much smaller presence, is one of the primary platforms on which Prime Minister Narendra Modi, Opposition leaders and other key political figures announce their policies, engage with each other and express their official positions on issues. WhatsApp, with a larger spread than any of the above, is perhaps the single largest medium for consumption of news— bigger than its sister platforms such as Facebook, but also, more importantly, bigger in its reach, perhaps, than any television channel, newspaper or online news publication.

Public Forums and Social Media

How online spaces such as Twitter and Facebook are regulated draws greatly from the laws on free speech. Internet platforms have tremendous power to shape and moderate content that they facilitate. Although they are run by private corporations, these platforms have become public squares for discourse without any public accountability, and have consequently blurred the lines between public and private. In the US, the Supreme Court have clearly held that streets and parks be kept open to the public for expressive activities. In the landmark case in 1939, Hague vs Committee for Industrial Organization, the court said clearly:

> Wherever the title of streets and parks may rest, they have immemorially been held in trust for the use of the public, and time out of mind, have been used for the purposes of assembly, communicating thoughts between citizens, and discussing public questions. Such use of the streets and public places has, from ancient times, been a part of the privileges, immunities, rights, and liberties of citizens.

The peculiarity of this privilege lies in that it moves beyond the limits of the state to penalize private actions that restrict the use of public property. As American constitutional law scholar Cass

Sunstein states, this means that free speech must be allowed to occur freely in public places, thus allowing citizens the right to assemble, protest and engage in free dialogue.[173] While we do not have anything similar to the public forum doctrine in India, we do have separately articulated rights to assembly, which may play similar functions in certain situations. However, this protection is not applicable to private spaces and will constitute encroachments into their property. Even privately owned spaces intended for assembly and gatherings such as hotels and restaurants do not come within the ambit of this right. A private owner of a commercial establishment has full discretion whether they allow their space for an event of gathering. With time, forums other than streets and parks have come to play the same role. If we want to reach out to others, it may be done more efficiently through a Facebook post than in the local community park. The more significant interchanges of ideas and the shaping of public consciousness may now be occurring over social media.

Yet, overall, courts globally have been resistant to accord the same status to the public forums on these platforms. The primary reason is that these remain privately owned platforms. They have their own community guidelines. Although often informed by the laws on issues such as copyright infringement, hate speech and misinformation, the guidelines are not judicially determined decisions.

This issue came up before the Southern District Court of New York in 2017 when the Twitter account of US President Donald Trump, @realDonaldTrump, blocked the accounts of seven US citizens. This meant that the seven Twitter accounts could not access the tweets of @realDonaldTrump. Those familiar with this handle would know that Trump, with his 63 million followers, uses Twitter daily to pronounce policy decisions and opinions. In fact, the White House Press Secretary, Sean Spencer, has clearly stated that the tweets were considered official statements by the president of the US.[174] Even though Twitter is a private party, does the argument of public forum still hold?

Rights guaranteed to us under the Constitution are either horizontal or vertical. Rights with vertical effects apply only against the government, whereas horizontal rights also apply against private actors. One of the key questions in any common law country is: To what extent are rights guaranteed under the Constitution enforceable against private actors? In most countries, including India and the US, the rights, barring a few exceptions, are only applicable against the government or where private parties are performing the functions of the government. But there could be situations where the rights also apply horizontally, either directly or indirectly.

In the case of tweets by President Trump, the court said that the interactive space accompanying each tweet, viz. how people are allowed to share, comment on and otherwise engage with the tweet, may be considered a designated public forum.[175] However, even here, the key thing was not whether Twitter was a public forum or not, but the fact that a citizen's right to access information by the government was being restricted. The reasoning is that the nature of the platform is irrelevant; it is the nature of the speech, and the fact that it is government speech, that is relevant.

This is, however, not the key conclusion according to me. Effectively, by holding Twitter as a public forum and striking down the use of its internal rules that allowed users to block others, the court emphasized how the internal guidelines of private platforms were subject to constitutional principles, notably the right to free speech and expression. Even though Donald Trump's is a private account and he operates it as any other private user, when the platform is used to perform roles that relate to public functions, it automatically transforms from a private account to a designated public forum.

In India, too, there have been several reported instances of public handles on Twitter blocking others. Apar Gupta, a lawyer and public policy professional, was blocked by the then Union Minister of State for Heavy Industries and Public Enterprises, Babul Supriyo. It would follow from the above reasoning that this was unconstitutional, as the right to freedom of speech and expression also includes the right to receive information. Gupta also argues in his blog that along with the right to speech and the right to receive information, with the advent of participative technologies, there must also be a third right, which is the right to interact (or the right to ping). This would be 'a legal basis for a citizen to reasonably convey a message to a public official. This can be on the basis of a message of a public official or even *suo motu* action. While such a right would not be a demand for attention, it would be the ability of a user to reach out to their social media profiles and not be blocked by them'.[176]

In the recent past, there have been other instances of blocking by Twitter handles of public offices and officials. Several Twitter users claimed that in early 2017, they were blocked by the @UIDAI handle. UIDAI has, however, denied this claim.[177]

Gupta's suggestion on the 'right to ping' opens the question of how activities on social media assume the character of public functions and come under the protection of rights. There is no additional protection granted to speech communicated in public forums in India. However, importantly, there is no limitation on the freedom of speech being extended to an individual communicating on private platforms. As indicated above, while fundamental rights are usually vertical in nature and do not apply to private parties, the rights may indirectly be horizontal. The state has the power to legislate limitations to the freedom of speech on the grounds of security of the state, the sovereignty and integrity of India, etc., but this does not mean that such rights can only be claimed against the state, or state functionaries.

The key functions of the public forum doctrine are to provide speakers with mass access to the general public. They not only allow access to potentially large numbers but also facilitate speakers to seek out the listeners. This doctrine is built on the notion that the availability of all speech on public forums for free could lead to the public being exposed to arguments and discourse related to issues of importance, and be driven to engage more with them, even through accidental encounters. In addition to such general access, the public forum also provides access to specific people. This form of access is often exercised by protests in front of a government body or building. In fact, this application of public forum is used often enough against private actors, such as a corporation or a commercial establishment, by using the public street without having to trespass on private property. Finally, the public forum also provides exposure, even if it is unwelcome, to a wide range of views and institutions.

It is gradually becoming clear that free speech and censorship work very differently on social media than it did when the public discourse was dominated by traditional media outlets controlling scarce broadcast and print resources. Turkish sociologist and author of *Twitter and Tear Gas: The Power and Fragility of Networked Protest*, Zeynep Tufecki, has argued that both the nature and the impact of censorship on social media are very different. Earlier, censorship acted by restricting speech. But in an age where there is a deluge of information, restricting speech is not the most effective form of censorship. It works in the form of organized harassment campaigns, which uses the qualities of a viral outrage to impose a disproportionate cost on the very act of speaking out. Therefore, censorship is not merely in the form of the removal of speech but is through disinformation and hate-speech campaigns. Both question the credibility of valid information sources but also distract through whataboutery and 'piecemeal leaks of hacked materials'.[178]

On 9 February 2016, students of Jawaharlal Nehru University (JNU) held a protest on their campus against the capital punishment awarded to Afzal Guru and Kashmiri separatist Maqbool Bhat for their roles in the 2001 terrorist attack on the Indian Parliament. The organizers of the event were former members of the Democratic Students Union. The students had received permission for the event, but it was withdrawn at the last minute due to objections raised by the Hindu nationalist student union Akhil Bharatiya Vidyarthi Parishad. Despite this, when the students went ahead with the protests, there were clashes between the two groups during the event. Curiously, a small group of individuals, wearing masks, whom a later investigation described as outsiders to the university, shouted 'anti-India' slogans.

Four days later, JNU Students Union President Kanhaiya Kumar was arrested by Delhi Police and charged with sedition. Two other students were arrested soon afterwards. In the media frenzy that followed, BJP spokesperson Sambit Patra played a doctored footage on his iPad which ostensibly showed Kumar shouting anti-India slogans.[179] This video, which was widely shared on social media and messaging groups, is a classic example of what Tufecki calls 'piecemeal leaks of hacked materials' and was instrumental in diverting the discussion from whether alleged sloganeering in a university campus even remotely qualified as one of the most serious speech offences in Indian law, which is punishable by life imprisonment.

The Chicago School and Weak Competition Laws

The amount of power that Internet giants such as Facebook, Google and Amazon are able to wield would not have been legally possible just a few decades ago. Before 1980, monopolies were considered bad for the economy in the US and were regulated much more heavily. This propensity to regulate monopolies goes back to Standard Oil in the 1880s. Standard Oil was leveraging its large market share in the refinery business to expand to other businesses. First, it began the backward integration into oil exploration and crude oil distribution. It soon followed it up with the forward integration into the retail distribution of its refined products to stores, and eventually, service stations throughout the US. It had used its scale to run its competitors out of business using lower pricing and threats to suppliers and distributors who did business with its competitor.

The Federal Trade Commission also emerged in response to the threats posed by monopolies in the US. Justice Louis Brandeis, who drove the antitrust movement in the US, believed that democracy hinged on the ability of citizens to control and check private concentrations of economic power. He saw the market as the ideal site for the exercise of individual liberty, and saw monopolies as threats to liberty. However, in the 1960s, another school of thought began emerging in law and economics, which argued that monopolies were generally efficient and pro-competitive so long as they did not lead to higher prices. This version of the antitrust law assessed competition primarily with a focus on the short-term interests of consumers. It paid less attention to the health of the market as a whole; antitrust doctrine views low consumer prices alone to be evidence of sound competition. This school of thought, popularly known as the Chicago school, was led by jurists such as Robert Bork, Richard Posner and Frank Easterbrook. This argument for a laissez-faire economic world was replete with Darwinian metaphors from evolutionary biology, arguing for the survival of the fittest, and Judge Easterbrook going on to famously state that, 'It is through the process of weeding out the weakest firms that the economy as a whole receives the greatest boost.' Since the Reagan era, the Chicago school became a default in antitrust policymaking in the US.

Contrast the post-Reagan era competition law with the peak years of antitrust after World War II. At that time, antitrust emerged almost as a strong democracy-enhancing ideology. The Americans were deeply suspicious of monopolies then as they viewed them as having directly enabled the rise of fascism in Germany. The German law had been tolerant of the rise of monopoly powers in arms, railroads and chemical industries. These businesses had backed Hitler when he was still trying to rally support. After the war, America went about enacting antitrust laws as intrinsic to the sustenance of a working democracy. This is best summed up in the words of Kennedy's antitrust chief, Lee Loevinger. When interviewing for the position with Robert Kennedy, the attorney general, in 1961, he said, 'I believe in antitrust almost as a secular religion.'[180]

On the other side of the Atlantic, a mirror movement towards strong antitrust laws emerged in Europe after the war. Led by a group called Ordoliberals from Germany, which had been oppressed by the Nazis, it also saw an economic concentration of power as contributing to the authoritarianism that the Nazis represented. By the 1960s, competition laws were seen as essential to a working democracy both in the US and Europe.

However, around this time, Aaron Director, who was teaching antitrust law at the University of Chicago, began articulating arguments that would form the basis of the Chicago school of antitrust. He critiqued the obsession with the need to preserve competition as an inefficient idea. Using traditional price theories, he began to argue that the artificial preservation of competition only sought to protect weaker, less efficient businesses from stronger, more efficient ones. In this quest for fostering competition, both the economy and 'consumer welfare' suffered. Director's emphasis on primacy of 'consumer welfare' had many followers, including federal judges Bork, Posner and Easterbrook, mentioned earlier.

Bit by bit, the Chicago school began to chip away at the legacy of the antitrust law solidified over the last few decades. The first low casualty was the 'per se' or categorical prohibitions in law. The US Supreme Court took a dim view of vertical integrations through arrangements between producers and retailers. It was left to Robert Bork to work towards a comprehensive alternative model for what the antitrust law should do. At the heart of Bork's conception was the 'consumer welfare' idea, which he claimed was always meant to be the primary goal of the antitrust law; its foremost indicator was lower prices. Bork published his treatise, 'The Antitrust Paradox', in 1964,[181] and followed it up with what was considered the single most influential academic paper in the field of antitrust law in the US—'Legislative Intent and Policy of the Sherman Act'.[182] From the fringe of suspect economic theory, Bork, with assistance from others, was able to turn the Chicago school into the default in American law and economics jurisprudence in less than two decades. The emergence of the Chicago school as the default in the American antitrust law played a large role in the unchecked dominance of a handful of Internet platforms emerging as monopolies.

The size of network power that the big technology firms control is unprecedented. Google drives 90 per cent of the Internet search;[183] 95 per cent of young adults on the Internet use some product owned by Facebook, and Amazon.com now accounts for 75 per cent of electronic book sales around the world. Apple and Microsoft Corp. supply 95 per cent of desktop operating systems, while 99 per cent of mobile phone operating systems are shared between Google and Apple.[184] Let us take the example of Amazon, which has benefitted from the largesse of the Chicago school most clearly. The company has been able to integrate vertically as well as horizontally.

To begin with, it had a market in non-perishable e-commerce goods. It began its horizontal integration by foraying into perishable goods with the purchase of Whole Foods,[185] and, more importantly, its cloud services business, Amazon Web Services. Its vertical integration has been more dramatic, involving the Marketplace, which incorporates third-party sellers; Basics, with Amazon private labels and bestselling commodity products; and hardware, such as Alexa voice-controlled devices and the Fire home video server.[186] Had Amazon existed in a pre-1980 world, its use of proprietary consumer data to identify, develop and sell products in direct competition with other sellers on its site would have attracted the attention of the Federal Trade Commission (FTC), and its distribution line would have been seen as an abuse of power. Similarly, its foray into perishable goods would have been problematic due to cross-subsidies. Even though we have not dealt with Amazon in any detail in this book, its reliance on lax anti-competition laws is a good place to understand how platforms have accumulated power.

It is interesting to look at the growth of Google. The company began with a search engine. Its search engine quickly emerged as a gateway to almost all activity on the Internet. Google used this advantage by offering free, easy-to-use and integrated alternatives to the services that had been created as a result of the web's open source community, as well as other large businesses. Thus, it gradually offered services in email, photos, maps, videos and productivity applications, to name a few.

In most cases, Google was in a position to leverage its benefits of monopoly power from an existing business to an emerging one. Yelp Inc., which, in 2004, began aggregating detailed information and user reviews of local services such as restaurants and stores, claims Google altered its search results to hurt Yelp and help its own competing service. After years of litigation, in 2017, the European Union (EU) found Google guilty of anti-competitive practices for its use of data from search engines and AdWords to destroy its European competition in the new price-comparison segment. The EU imposed a fine of $2.7 billion on Google, but this judgement was also possible primarily because it was possible to demonstrate obvious harm in this case. In other cases of predatory platform behaviour, it has proven to be more difficult.

Earlier anti-competitive policies only allowed companies to either create markets or participate in them, but they could not play both roles. By having a creator of the market also participate, there would be an unfair and inherent advantage. The Chicago school's benevolent view of monopolies allows Facebook and Google to both create markets and be participants. When Google acquired DoubleClick, it was essentially acquiring a means to influence a market in which it was already a participant. It allowed Google to favour its own businesses in the online advertising space through its use of DoubleClick. Similarly, Google's purchase of YouTube was the acquisition of a new market, which enabled it to tweak the YouTube algorithms to give preferential treatment to its own content on the platform.

Economists call these kinds of examples 'two-sided markets'. In this, there are two distinct user groups that, when brought together, provide each other with network benefits. Consumers are both the source of data and the product. The advertisers are the customers; they provide the market's revenue and depend on the scale of the market. The kind of scale that Facebook and Google enjoy provides advantages that are irreversible in a competitive system without interventions. The combination of its search engine, cloud services and venture capital business provides Google with a unique view of the new products and services. Its use of this market power to accumulate either through acquisition or by driving competitors out of business is not unlawful under the Chicago school of antitrust, so long as it does not translate into high prices for the consumers.

Facebook imitated Google's model of usurping the open webspace. It began with the social networking business, but soon acquired Instagram to capture the online photo- and video-sharing market. It kept using its Messenger and acquired WhatsApp to acquire a large share of the online messaging market, and also forayed into virtual reality with Oculus. Unlike Google, Facebook's model has been to focus on the content market. It has done this by offering publishers products such as Instant Articles. It also acquired the now extinct virtual private network application, Onavo. All of these businesses provide Facebook with valuable consumer data, which fuels its targeted advertising business. But with Onavo, Facebook also tracks its competitors very closely. Apple had disqualified Onavo for violation of its privacy standards, and was withdrawn from its app store. Similarly, Facebook's predatory behaviour against Snapchat, which it has sought to acquire for a few years now, would also have attracted penalty from a robust competition law.

India's competition law is much more recent than that of the US. In fact, the Sherman Antitrust Act in the US existed a good seventy-seven years before India even gained independence. The first Indian legislation to govern monopolies and competition was the Monopolies and Restrictive Trade Practices Act of 1969. This was later repealed and replaced by the Competition Act. The current version of the competition law goes back to 2002, which primarily prohibits an agreement 'which causes or is likely to cause an appreciable adverse effect on competition within India'. Much like the US Post Law 1980, it prohibits specific types of monopolies—agreements to determine price, agreements to limit supply, agreements to share a market and agreements to engage in collusive bidding. While the capacity of the Indian state and law to hold giant technology platforms accountable for anti-competitive practices on its own is suspect, there is a clear need for the global reform of the competition law.

Unlike the previous instances of monopolies colluding with states to undermine democracy, technology platforms do not back autocrats in quite the same way. Yet, their dominance does offer opportunities for authoritarian regimes to leverage them for manipulation and control over narratives. The record of the large technology companies in taking positions on human rights issues is also suspect. The limited experience of Google trying to take on the Chinese government shows the moral flexibility of the large technology companies. When Google was initially introduced in China, it positioned itself as the company with the motto 'Don't be evil'. When Chinese users searched for censored content on Google.cn, they saw a notice that some results had been removed. This public acknowledgement of censorship in China was a small victory for transparency. On 12 January 2010, Google announced, 'We have decided we are no longer willing to continue censoring our results on Google.cn, and so, over the next few weeks, we will be discussing with the Chinese government the basis on which we could operate an unfiltered search engine within the law, if at all'.[187] The Chinese response was to block Facebook, Twitter and Google's YouTube in one go. In 2014, they blocked all of the major services of Google in China. Over the last years, there have been several reports about Google working on a clandestine censored search engine for China.[188]

In India, too, there have been several allegations levelled at platforms such as Facebook of 'censoring' content that is critical of the ruling dispensation. In August 2018, *Caravan*, an Indian magazine which has published several investigative stories questioning members of the ruling party, had published an article on the financial discrepancies in the assets declared by a senior BJP leader. They wanted to boost this article on Facebook. However, they had to wait for an inordinately long time to get Facebook to boost the post, even though they had a verified account on

Facebook.[189] Similarly, a few journalists who were critical of the government complained that they were being locked out of their Facebook accounts for no explicable reason.[190]

A Short History of Piddling Commitments

Facebook

In his testimony before the US Congress in April 2018, Zuckerberg promised to take steps before the US general elections to report political advertising and curb misinformation. He also committed to getting this done in time before the elections in Mexico, Brazil, India and Pakistan. Consequently, five days later, a little less than a month before the Karnataka state assembly elections, Facebook announced a partnership with BoomLive, an independent Mumbai-based fact-checking organization that was certified by the International Fact-Checking Network to fight misinformation during the Karnataka assembly polls. The press release had promised that once a story was rated as false, Facebook was able to reduce its distribution by 80 per cent, and thereby improve the accuracy of the information on the platform and reduce misinformation.[191]

However, in an election cycle that attracted more than its fair share of attention for misinformation, fake polls and surveys, communally coloured rumours and blatant lies, Facebook, along with BoomLive, was able to debunk only thirty stories of misinformation on its platform—twenty-five in the run-up to the polls and five in the immediate aftermath. From the beginning of the election cycle, false statements by prominent politicians— including the ministers in the government—were an everyday affair. As is now the norm, they were faithfully reported by most media outlets without critique or context.[192] Misinformation masquerading as opinion, wherein a set of legitimate facts are presented out of context to arrive at a blatantly false conclusion, was also a persistent feature during the polls. The much-publicized initiative eventually translated into a small financial commitment from Facebook and allowed BoomLive to hire exactly two fact-checkers—one based in its office in Mumbai and another on the ground in Karnataka. Further, Facebook offered little by way of support to BoomLive.[193]

Govindraj Ethiraj, founder and editor of BoomLive, said Facebook's contribution to their fact-checking efforts was very limited, and they had to rely on their own conventional methods of tracking misinformation. This involved methods of limited means—asking friends and family to forward anything suspicious they came across, maintaining their WhatsApp helpline for users to direct suspicious-looking links, and monitoring pages known to be potential sources of misinformation. Jency Jacobs, the managing editor of BoomLive, talked about how it took a couple of people working all day to fact-check a single video. BoomLive, with only six fact-checkers, including the two Facebook-funded hires, could act on only a fraction of the tip-offs.

With greater pressure, in the run-up to the 2019 general elections, Facebook took down several pages for 'coordinated inauthentic behaviour', which included 687 pages and accounts linked to the Congress and a smaller but far more influential number of what appeared to be pro-BJP accounts.[194] Facebook set up a 'war room' to monitor content regarding elections in India at its headquarters in Menlo Park, composed of 'information warriors' to watch out for hoaxes, voter-suppression attempts, suspicious account behaviour, hate messages, fake accounts and spikes in spam. In India, they tied up with seven fact-checking organizations to monitor content in English, Hindi, Bengali, Marathi, Telugu, Tamil, Malayalam and Gujarati. It was reported that Facebook had assembled forty cross-disciplinary teams, 'drawn from areas like cybersecurity, public policy, data science, legal, engineering, threat intelligence, research and others to work together in sync at the command centre to co-ordinate, detect and respond to situations in real time'.[195] As they have been promising for a few years, Facebook is reportedly deploying machine-learning-based automated tools to block or remove approximately one million accounts a day. The automated tools are supposed to help identify abusive content or content violating policy of usage at scale, and quickly locate it across the platform and remove it in bulk, before it has a chance to spread. Facebook also added twenty-four new languages, including sixteen languages from India, to its automatic translation system.

WhatsApp

Over the last year, there has been a series of demands from the Indian government for WhatsApp to build traceability for its messages so as to detect where the misinformation or other problematic content is originating from. The Ministry of Electronics and Information Technology has so far sent two notices to WhatsApp. In the first notice, the ministry said that the instances of lynchings were 'because of large number of irresponsible and explosive messages filled with rumours and provocations being circulated on WhatsApp', and directed WhatsApp to use technology to prevent these messages from spreading, and to 'take immediate action to end this menace'. If only it were so easy! As unwise as it is for the ministry to blame lynchings on a technology company without considering the underlying social issues as well as the complicity of its own government and party in enabling such incidents, it is, however, worthwhile to consider the steps that WhatsApp can take. In a second notice, the ministry demanded that WhatsApp come up with 'effective solutions' and 'facilitate enforcement of law', and build traceability. WhatsApp has so far resisted the suggestion of building any form of traceability, claiming that it would compromise its end-to-end encryption framework and endanger consumer privacy.

Overall, WhatsApp's current approach to addressing the problems on its platforms are restricted to training its algorithms to detect 'how' messages are shared and made to go viral, rather than 'what' messages are shared. These could include paying attention to 'span farms' where they play a role in disseminating misinformation or hate speech. It has also reportedly sent 'cease and desist letters' to marketing firms on mass messaging.

More notably, in 2018, it announced restrictions on forwarding. Earlier, the platform allowed a user to send a hundred forwards in one go. WhatsApp reduced that number to five in India and to twenty for the rest of the world. It also introduced a 'forwarded' label on messages to help people identify that the message is not directly from the sender, and that they are only circulating a message shared by someone else.

The company also disabled the 'quick forward' option next to media messages (photos and videos) and introduced a 'suspicious link' label for URLs that its algorithm could detect contained unusual characters. There has been limited development on this end, and progress on analysis of suspicious URLs for misinformation or hate speech has been slow.

These strategies have had little impact, as political campaigns have found ways to circumvent the limitations posed by them. In April 2019, Huffington Post reported that a Jaipur-based private company, Sarv Webs Pvt. Ltd, was being used by the ruling party to spread messages on WhatsApp. According to the reports, the company maintains a large number of SIM cards, and uses multiple numbers to send messages on WhatsApp. As there is a restriction on the number of participants in a WhatsApp group, each number is used to set up several groups. They kept close tabs on the number of WhatsApp groups each of these phone numbers were part of, and the number of messages sent, received and read by group members. They also tracked the number of replies to their messages and how engaged recipients are.[196] This is not limited to one company or one party, as other political parties have realized the efficacy of WhatsApp as a medium too.

WhatsApp also allows all members of a group to collect the mobile numbers of all of the other members of the group. As Indian laws require all mobile numbers to be registered, it presents opportunities for the ruling party in a state to identify both its supporters and detractors from their presence in ideologically aligned WhatsApp groups, or by using volunteers to join WhatsApp to identify party loyalties based on the messages of users on a group.

Just weeks before the general elections in 2019, WhatsApp launched a new fact-checking service in India. This allowed WhatsApp users to forward messages to the Checkpoint Tipline, where a team led by local start-up Proto assessed and marked them as either 'true', 'false', 'misleading' or 'disputed'. However, several users pointed out that it took very long for WhatsApp to verify the contents of a message after it had been reported.[197]

Proto itself accepted that this would have limited impact on fighting the misinformation ecosystem in India ahead of the election. It was entirely dependent on users voluntarily submitting messages for feedback, and would do little, if anything at all, to address the consumption by those inclined to believe in the information, and therefore, unlikely to report it. They themselves noted that the ultimate aim was to 'study the misinformation phenomenon at scale' so that they could help WhatsApp identify the issues, regions and languages most likely to be affected. This was indeed far too little, far too late.

Twitter

Twitter's responses to the amount of political misinformation were even more lukewarm. On 24 April 2019, after three phases of polling were over, it introduced a feature that allowed users to report posts attempting to 'undermine the process of registering to vote or engaging in the electoral process'. A Twitter blog post from April 2019 named 'Strengthening Our Approach to Deliberate Attempts to Mislead Voters' announced the very limited function of these features, which was to report misleading information specifically about the process of voting, registration, identification and dates. The last day for registration for a voter ID card was over well before these features were launched. More importantly, this feature was only limited to the very specific form of misinformation about the process of voting, and did not address the huge scale of the problem of political misinformation that existed on the platform.[198]

The Road Ahead

The scale of the extreme-speech problem that exists online is a testament to the fact that the safe harbour framework has run its course. Two alternatives to this system have emerged in the last few years—either the law can mandate regulation, or it can prescribe guidelines on the basis of which platforms can regulate information.

The first approach, of imposing statutory liability on web platforms for harmful speech, is widely criticized for being violative of the constitutionally protected human right of free speech and expression. Because private platforms operate with the fear of being penalized if they fail to regulate harmful speech, they are likely to err on the side of caution and remove content, even when it is unnecessary. This can have a chilling effect on free speech on the Internet. This threat to free speech is exacerbated by the difficulty in enforcing such regulatory policies. Regulations expect platforms to take down content within a prescribed time period from the time they have 'knowledge' of the objectionable content. For platforms with millions of users, all with the ability to post and report content, having short time periods, such as twenty-four hours, for takedown of content poses a very heavy burden. The natural response that platforms will have would be to remove content, without diligently evaluating its illegality.

The second approach is that of a more involved form of co-regulation. For example, the German law that seeks to implement hate speech online, the Network Enforcement Law, envisions the recognition of independent institutions as self-regulated ones within the purview of the Act. Where certain content is reported by users as illegal, but the same is not manifestly unlawful, the service provider is permitted up to seven days to remove it; here, the provider may refer the decision of unlawfulness to this self-regulated institution. The idea of having trusted institutions such as press councils play a more active role is a good one. However, the German framework compromises the independence of the institutions significantly. It allows the Federal Office of Justice the power to 'recognize' institutions. Ideally, this power should be fully independent of the State, and should include representation from stakeholders from within the industry and civil society.

Both approaches have their own pros and cons, and perhaps a responsive regulatory approach that identifies behaviour incentives and disincentives for good and bad behaviour by the range of actors is necessary. It would also be completely futile to imagine that simply regulating Internet platforms is the key. More robust regulation of political advertising and paid content on these platforms is necessary. However, more traditional regulations, such as reforming campaign finance laws, are needed. According to the report of election watchdog Association for Democratic Reforms, in 2017–18 India's seven largest political parties received ₹1,397.90 crore in all. Out of this, the BJP alone received ₹1,027.34 crore, out of which ₹989 crores were from donations.[199] More than 50 per cent of all party funds were from unknown sources. This was made possible, at least in some part, by the electoral bonds that permit donors, including foreign parties, to make anonymous tax-free contributions. Out of the ₹222 crore worth of electoral bonds purchased in 2017–18, ₹210 crore went to the BJP.[200] When a ruling party can create policies designed to benefit it, it can, under the guise of a public mandate, very quickly skew the playing field against other parties. There is a dire need to find ways to regulate the funding of more diffuse actors who, without formal affiliations to political outfits, play the role of able-footed soldiers.

The move from full-blooded coups to democratic backsliding means that democracies erode gradually rather than implode rapidly. If we have to have any chance of arresting this slide, it is important to recognize that current trends are not random events but natural responses to local and international incentives. The opportunities for dissemination of unchecked information offered by social media and online messaging platforms as they become primary sources of information for people is a significant factor. The concentration of power in these platforms may not manifest as support for authoritarian regimes as directly as they did in the pre-World War II era. Yet, our short history of experience with these platforms shows that without aligning themselves with autocratic figures, their information flow has offered unique opportunities to polarize people through racially and religiously charged content, manipulating people's understandings of their political reality by using misinformation campaigns effectively, and subverting the nature of political discourse through organized extreme speech and online harassment.

The decay in democratic processes, while a response to systemic incentives, is also not something that comes about on its own. There is always a strategic design and agency that brings about this decay. Even in the case of diffuse actors who may operate without the clear authorization of their political masters, they are responding to a clear call for arms, and when they go beyond the remit of their brief, it is but merely the logical next step for them.

So far, the response to these problems has been limited to how the law, in its current form, or in a form that it needs to evolve into, addresses them. This places the ball squarely in the judiciary's court to adjudicate on legal and constitutional questions. Any effective solution to a problem should give capacity and agency to those who have most to lose if the problem comes to pass. The possible strengthening of competition law to curb the monopolies of Internet platforms is one potential response, so that we have a competing economy where the attention of the public is not limited to a few large actors.

As we discussed at the beginning of the book, the irrational public is easily compromised and manipulated. It is futile to lament the failures of democracy when the public fails to achieve the impossible levels of 'omnicompetence' that Lippmann saw as the basis of democracies. It is similarly pointless to infantilize the public and see them as a passive recipient of information—both legitimate and illegitimate—and then change their beliefs, opinions and actions in response to them. The public, while irrational, is complex in how it reacts to information. When we do get manipulated by polarizing speech, it is a symptom of a deeper underlying social problem. To focus our energies simply on the specific message that led us to irrational actions, whether in the form of voting against our own interests or engaging in mob violence, would be pointless. Perhaps Dewey's ideal of the public's social existence, and the ability to form associations, is where we need to look. The way a democracy can work is if the public can organize itself in a way that it can use the information that it drew from its social environment to inform its collective action. This would require a competitive market where the public can choose its sources of information and recognize privately owned platforms as public forums and have meaningful mechanisms to engage and associate with.

Acknowledgements

The idea for this book evolved over conversations with several colleagues and friends, and their questions, insights and provocations. For the last few years, I have been blessed with supervisors who have given me both the support and flexibility to pursue this book—Sunil Abraham, for his ready generosity with time, ideas and acuity; Sumandro Chattapadhyay, for always asking the difficult questions and making me reevaluate my arguments; and Elonnai Hickok, for giving me the enviable opportunity to work on issues, connected yet diverse. At work, my understanding of subjects that make their way into this book has been enriched by discussions with colleagues and friends—most notably Rakhi Sehgal, Saikat Datta, Yesha Tshering Paul, Hans Varghese Mathews and Srinivas Kodali.

My thinking on several issues in this book has been guided by leading scholars, both current and past. My views on liberal democracies, propaganda and the role of the public have been shaped, to begin with, by the rich and abiding discourse in the Lippmann-Dewey debates. Other scholars that have guided the thinking in this book include Jürgen Habermas, Hannah Arendt, Daniel Kahnemann, Jack Balkin, danah boyd, Cass Sunstein, Tim Wu, Rahul Verma, Pradeep Chhibber, Chinmayi Arun, Tarunabh Khaitan, Ramachandra Guha and Zeynep Tufecki. Several recent books and investigative reports on political targeting in India and abroad have played a role in informing the arguments in this book, including works by Shivam Shankar Singh, Eitan Hersh, Shivam Vij and Ullekh NP.

I thank the entire team at Rupa for their support through the process of writing this book. Additionally, I would also like to thank Anishka Vaishnav for her help with the references in this book.

Being able to write a book is an act of privilege and luxury, even at the worst of times, and is only made possible due to our circumstances and the contribution of several people who enable us to do so. My interest in reading and writing owes a debt of gratitude to the literary interests and expansive library of my late uncle, Vidyapati Nath Sinha. It was the many childhood hours spent in his study that evoked an interest in history and politics in me, and eventually led me to an education in Humanities. My parents, Chanda and Basant Sinha, have given me opportunities and support, at times, at great personal expense, for which I am truly grateful. What perhaps makes their contribution even more selfless is their support even when they may not have agreed with, or fully understood my decisions. Thanks also to Prateek for withstanding a full week of my simultaneous need for both single-minded concentration for writing and distractions from writing, and other friends and family for humouring me through the process.

Finally, and foremost, this book owes more than anyone else to my partner, Pooja, who has not only supported my life in public policy and writing, both emotionally and financially, but also convinced me to write this book. Her tangible contributions to this book were truly significant—editing, detailed notes on structure and rewrites, typesetting and cover design, but it were the less tangible contributions of timely words of encouragement, and a show of faith, which helped me the most.

Endnotes

1. Graber, Mark A., Sanford Levinson, and Mark V. Tushnet, *Constitutional Democracy in Crisis?* New York: Oxford University Press, 2018.
2. Foa, Roberto Stefan and Yascha Mounk, 'The Signs of Deconsolidation', *Journal of Democracy* 28 (2017): 5.
3. Bermeo, Nancy, 'On Democratic Backsliding', *Journal of Democracy* 27 (2016): 5–19.
4. Kurlantzick, Joshua, *Democracy in Retreat: The Revolt of the Middle Class and the Worldwide Decline of Representative Government*, New Haven: Yale University Press, 2014.
5. Huq, Aziz Z. and Tom Ginsburg, 'How to Lose a Constitutional Democracy', *UCLA Law Review* 65 (2018): 78, 83.
6. Barber, Sotirios A., *Constitutional Failure*, Lawrence: University Press of Kansas, 2014.
7. Balkin, Jack M., 'Constitutional Crisis and Constitutional Rot', *Constitutional Democracy in Crisis?* New York: Oxford University Press, 2018.
8. Dahl, Robert, *On Democracy*, New Haven: Yale University Press, 1999.
9. Law, David and Chien-Chih Lin, 'Constitutional Inertia in Asia', *Constitutional Democracy in Crisis?* New York: Oxford University Press, 2018.
10. Udupa, Sahana, 'India Needs a Fresh Strategy to Tackle Online Extreme Speech', *Economic and Political Weekly*, 11 February 2019, accessed 26 July 2019, https://www.epw.in/engage/article/election-2019-india-needs-fresh-strategy-to-tackle-new-digital-tools.
11. IANS, 'We May Cease to Exist in India If New Regulations Kick In:

WhatsApp', *The Economic Times*, 6 February 2019, https://economictimes.indiatimes.com/tech/internet/we-may-cease-to-exist-in-india-if-new-regulations-kick-in-whatsapp/articleshow/67870455.cms.
12. Lippmann, Walter, *The Phantom Public*, New Brunswick: Transaction Publishers, 1925.
13. Achen, Christopher H. and Larry M. Bartels, *Democracy for Realists: Why Elections Do Not Produce Responsive Government*, Princeton University Press, 2016.
14. Dewey, John, *The Public and Its Problems*, USA: Henry Holt and Company, 1927.
15. Matthews, Roderick, *The Great Indian Rope Trick: Does the Future of Democracy Lie with India?* Hachette India, 2015.
16. Rudolph, Lloyd and Sussane Hoeber Rudolph, *In Pursuit of Lakshmi: The Political Economy of the Indian State*, University of Chicago Press Books, 1987.
    'Party System and Party Politics in India', *ICSSR Research Surveys and Explorations: Political Science*, Volume 2: Indian Democracy, edited by K. C. Suri and Achin Vanaik, 209–52, New Delhi: Oxford University Press, 2013.
17. Guha, Ramachandra, 'The Absent Liberal: An Essay on Politics and Intellectual Life', *Economic and Political Weekly* 36, no. 50 (15 December 2001): 4663-670, https://www.epw.in/journal/2001/50/special-articles/absent-liberal.html.
18. Kaviraj, Sudipta, *The Enchantment of Democracy and India: Politics and Ideas*, Orient Blackswan, 2012.
19. Mehta, Pratap Bhanu, *The Burden of Democracy*, New Delhi: Penguin Books, 2003.
20. Chhibber, Pradeep K. and Verma, Rahul, *Ideology and Identity*, Oxford University Press.
21. Bayly, C.A., *Recovering Liberties: Indian Thought in the Age of Liberalism and Empire*, Cambridge University Press, 2011.
22. Chhibber, Pradeep K. and Verma, Rahul, *Ideology and Identity*, Oxford University Press.
23. Sen, Amartya, *The Argumentative Indian: Writings on Indian History, Culture and Identity*, Penguin UK, 1st edition, 2006.
24. 'Functioning of 16th Lok Sabha (2014-2019)', PRS Legislative Research,

https://www.prsindia.org/parliamenttrack/vital-stats/functioning-16th-lok-sabha-2014-2019.
25. Silverman, Craig and Lawrence Alexander, 'How Teens in the Balkans Are Duping Trump Supporters with Fake News', BuzzFeed News, 2016, available at https://www.buzzfeednews.com/article/craigsilverman/how-macedonia-became-a-global-hub-for-pro-trump-misinfo.
26. 'Gartner Reveals Top Predictions for IT Organizations and Users in 2018 and Beyond', Gartner, Accessed 9 August, 2019, https://www.gartner.com/en/newsroom/press-releases/2017-10-03-gartner-reveals-top-predictions-for-it-organizations-and-users-in-2018-and-beyond.
27. Kashatus, William C., 'This Was a Real 'Fake News' Story—and It Landed Us in a War', History News Network (Columbian College of Arts & Sciences), 26 February 2018, https://historynewsnetwork.org/article/168374.
28. 'The Corpse Factory and the Birth of Fake News', The British Broadcasting Corporation, 17 February 2017, https://www.bbc.com/news/entertainment-arts-38995205.
29. Pariser, Eli, *The Filter Bubble Penguin Books*, Reprint Edition, 2012.
30. Farooqui, Mahmood, *Besieged: Voices from Delhi 1857*, New Delhi: Penguin Global, 2012.
31. Carey Library and Katharine Smith Diehl, *Early Indian Imprints: an Exhibition from the William Carey Historical Library of Serampore*, Serampore: Council of Serampore College, 1962.
32. Arendt, Hannah, *Crises of the Republic: Lying in Politics; Civil Disobedience; On Violence; Thoughts on Politics and Revolution*, New York: Harcourt Brace Jovanovich, 1972.
33. Giglietto, Fabio, Laura Lannelli, Luca Rossi and Augusto Valeriani, 'Fakes, News and the Election: A New Taxonomy for the Study of Misleading Information Within the Hybrid Media System', The SSRN, 17 April 2019, https://papers.ssrn.com/sol3/papers.cfm?abstract_id=2878774.
34. Wardle, Claire and Hossein Derakhshan,' Information Disorder: Toward an Interdisciplinary Framework for Research and Policy Making', Council of Europe Report DGI (2017) 09, Council of Europe, 2017.
35. Jack, Caroline, 'Lexicon of Lies: Terms for Problematic Information', Data & Society, September 8 2017, https://datasociety.net/output/lexicon-of-lies/.

36. Bhushan, Sandeep, *The Indian Newsroom*, Context Publishing Company, 2019.
37. Sidharth, Arjun, 'Fake Quotes by Global Leaders Praising PM Modi Circulate on Social Media', AltNews.in, 17 May 2018, https://www.altnews.in/fake-quotes-by-global-leaders-praising-pm-modi-circulate-on-social-media/.
38. Sinha, Pratik, 'BUSTED: 'True' Story by Manish Malhotra about Modi Working 18–20 Hours a Day', AltNews.in, 9 March 2017, https://www.altnews.in/busted-true-story-manish-malhotra-modi-working-18-20-hours-day/.
39. Indo-Asian News Service, 'UNESCO Declares Modi Best Prime Minister: Top 10 Fake News That We (almost) Believed in 2016', *India Today*, 26 December 2016, https://www.indiatoday.in/india/story/top-ten-fake-news-that-we-almost-believed-in-2016-modi-best-pm-declared-unesco-359619-2016-12-26.
40. Patel, Jignesh, 'Fake News: Alok Verma Called PM Modi "Most Corrupt Prime Minister in Independent India" in His Resignation Letter', AltNews.in, 12 January 2019, https://www.altnews.in/fake-news-alok-verma-called-pm-modi-most-corrupt-prime-minister-in-independent-india-in-his-resignation-letter/.
41. 'FAKE ALERT: Surveys Declaring PM Modi, Congress Corrupt Are Fake', *The Times of India*, 17 September 2018, https://timesofindia.indiatimes.com/news/fake-alert-bbc-has-nothing-to-do-with-surveys-declaring-pm-modi-congress-corrupt/articleshow/65840015.cms.
42. Balkrishna, 'Fact Check: Was Modi Right about Congress Leaders Not Meeting Bhagat Singh in Jail?' *India Today*, 18 September 2018, https://www.indiatoday.in/fact-check/story/fact-check-was-modi-right-about-congress-leaders-not-meeting-bhagat-singh-in-jail-1231140-2018-05-10.
43. 'Chennai Floods: Edited Modi Photo Sparks Online Mockery', The British Broadcasting Corporation, 4 December 2015, https://www.bbc.com/news/world-asia-india-34991822.
44. 'Relax, PM Modi's Complimentary FIFA Jersey Says "G20", Not "420"', The Quint, 3 December 2018, https://www.thequint.com/news/webqoof/modis-fifa-jersey-says-g20-and-not-420.
45. 'In Annual Report, Home Ministry Confuses Spain-Morocco Border for

India-Pakistan Border', Firstpost, 15 June 2017, https://www.firstpost.com/india/home-ministry-goofs-up-in-annual-report-uses-spain-Morocco-border-picture-for-india-pakistan-border-3645981.html.
46. Chaudhuri, Pooja, 'Was Nehru Thrashed by a Mob in 1962 after 'failure on China War'?' AltNews.in, 14 September 2018, https://www.altnews.in/was-nehru-thrashed-by-a-mob-in-1962-after-failure-on-china-war/.
47. Chaudhuri, Pooja, 'Media Analysis: RSS-affiliated Org Reported as 'Muslim Women' Supporting Ram Mandir in Ayodhya', AltNews.in, 27 November 2018, https://www.altnews.in/media-analysis-rss-affiliated-org-reported-as-muslim-women-supporting-ram-mandir-in-ayodhya/.
48. 'It's Come to This, Fake News Website Claims PM Modi Has Deposited Rs 15 Lakh in Every Account', DailyO.in, 4 October 2017, https://www.dailyo.in/variety/modi-deposit-rs-15-lakh-fake-postcard-news-economy-demonetisation/story/1/19875.html.
49. 'Watch: BJP Has "Lust to Divide", Says Trinamool MP Mahua Moitra in a Fiery Maiden Speech', Scroll.in, 26 June 2019, Accessed 25 July 2019, https://scroll.in/video/928366/watch-bjp-has-lust-to-divide-says-trinamool-mp-mahua-moitra-in-a-fiery-maiden-speech.
50. Arora, Nishant, 'Is Internet Usage in India Being Calculated in Right Way?' *Mint*, 8 March 2019, https://www.livemint.com/industry/infotech/is-internet-usage-in-india-being-calculated-in-right-way-1552054425030.html.
51. Pariser, Eli, *The Filter Bubble*, Penguin Books, Reprint Edition, 2012.
52. Singh, Shivam Shankar, *How to Win an Indian Election: What Political Parties Don't Want You to Know*, Penguin Ebury Press, 2019.
53. Beauchamp, Zack, 'These Charts Show How Social Media Makes the Israel-Palestine Debate Worse', Vox, 7 April 2014. https://www.vox.com/2014/8/7/5971759/chart-israel-palestine-polarized-twitter.
54. boyd, danah, 'Streams of Content, Limited Attention: The Flow of Information through Social Media', Web2.0 Expo, 17 November 2009, http://www.danah.org/papers/talks/Web2Expo.html.
55. Bakshi, Eytan, Messing Solomon, Lada Adamic, 'Exposure to Ideologically Diverse News and Opinion on Facebook', Facebook Research, 9 May 2015, available at https://research.fb.com/publications/exposure-to-ideologically-diverse-information-on-facebook/

56. Srinivasan, Dina, 'The Antitrust Case Against Facebook', *Berkeley Business Law Journal* Vol. 16, Issue 1, Forthcoming, 10 September 2018, https://ssrn.com/abstract=3247362
57. Gerlitz, Carolin and Anne Helmond, 'The Like Economy: Social Buttons and the Data-Intensive Web', *New Media & Society* 15, no. 8 (April 2013): 1348–65, https://doi.org/10.1177/1461444812472322.
58. https://core.ap.gov.in/CMDASHBOARD/SiteMapReport.aspx.
59. Zuckerberg, Mark, 'Understanding Facebook's Business Model', Facebook Newsroom, 24 January 2019, https://newsroom.fb.com/news/2019/01/understanding-facebooks-business-model/
60. 'WhatsApp 2019: Stats and Facts', 1 February 2019, https://99firms.com/blog/whatsapp-statistics/
61. 'Number of Monthly Active WhatsApp Users in India from August 2013 to February 2017 (in Millions)', Statista, 8 May 2019, https://www.statista.com/statistics/280914/monthly-active-whatsapp-users-in-india/.
62. Jayarajan, Sreedevi, 'TN Horror: Mob Mistakes 65-year-old Woman for Child Trafficker, Lynches Her to Death', The News Minute, 10 May 2018, https://www.thenewsminute.com/article/tn-horror-mob-mistakes-65-year-old-woman-child-trafficker-lynches-her-death-81010.
63. Ibid.
64. Dixit, Pranav, 'How WhatsApp Destroyed a Village', BuzzFeed News, 7 November 2018, accessed 30 July 2019, https://www.buzzfeednews.com/article/pranavdixit/whatsapp-destroyed-village-lynchings-rainpada-india.
65. '"He Looked like a Terrorist": How a Drive in Karnataka Ended in Mob Lynching', *Hindustan Times*, 30 July 2018, accessed 25 July 2019, https://www.hindustantimes.com/india-news/he-looked-like-a-terrorist-how-a-drive-in-rural-india-ended-in-a-mob-attack-and-a-lynching/story-48MpOGGkqjbDwgv3eigOwJ.html.
66. 'Mentally Challenged Homeless Woman Lynched by Mob over Child Lifting Rumours in Madhya Pradesh', *The New Indian Express*, accessed 25 July 2019, http://www.newindianexpress.com/nation/2018/jul/23/mentally-challenged-homeless-woman-lynched-by-mob-over-child-lifting-rumours-in-madhya-pradesh-1847404.html.
67. Saikia, Arunabh, '"Everything That Could Go Wrong Went Wrong":

Days of Rumours Led to the Lynchings in Assam Village', Scroll.in, 12 June 2018, Accessed 25 July 2019, https://scroll.in/article/882265/everything-that-could-go-wrong-went-wrong-days-of-rumours-led-to-the-lynchings-in-assam-village.

68. 'Woman Lynched, 3 Injured on Suspicion of Child Lifting in Ahmedabad', News18, 27 June 2018, accessed 25 July 2019, https://www.news18.com/news/india/woman-beggar-lynched-on-suspicion-of-child-lifting-in-ahmedabad-1791631.html.

69. 'Two Migrant Labourers Assaulted in Tamil Nadu on Suspicion of Being Child Lifters', News18, 1 July 2018, accessed 25 July 2019, https://www.news18.com/news/india/two-migrant-workers-mistaken-for-child-lifters-beaten-up-in-tamil-nadu-1797125.html.

70. 'Jiyapally Lynching: 6 Villagers Arrested', *The Times of India*, accessed 25 July 2019, https://timesofindia.indiatimes.com/city/hyderabad/jiyapally-lynching-6-villagers-arrested/articleshow/64317625.cms.

71. Khanna, Pretika, Abhiram Ghadyalpatil, Shaswati Das, 'Death by Social Media', *LiveMint*, 9 July 2018, accessed 25 July 2019, https://www.livemint.com/Politics/jkSPTSf6IJZ5vGC1CFVyzI/Death-by-Social-Media.html.

72. https://www.thehindu.com/news/national/karnataka/after-rumours-northeast-people-flee-bangalore/article3776549.ece.

73. 'Fact Finding Report: Independent Inquiry into Muzaffarnagar "Riots"', *Economic and Political Weekly*, 3 January 2014, accessed 25 July 2019, https://www.epw.in/journal/2014/2/reports-states-web-exclusives/fact-finding-report-independent-inquiry-muzaffarnagar.

74. Arun, Chinmayi, 'On WhatsApp, Rumours, and Lynchings', *Economic and Political Weekly*, 11 February 2019, accessed 25 July 2019, https://www.epw.in/journal/2019/6/insight/whatsapp-rumours-and-lynchings.html.

75. TNN & Agencies, 'Union Minister Jayant Sinha Garlands 8 Lynching Convicts, Faces Opposition Flak', *The Times of India*, accessed 25 July 2019, https://timesofindia.indiatimes.com/india/union-minister-jayant-sinha-garlands-8-lynching-convicts-faces-opposition-flak/articleshow/64901863.cms.

76. 'WhatsApp Appoints Grievance Officer to Curb Fake News in India', *LiveMint*, 23 September 2018, accessed 26 July 2019, https://www.livemint.com/Companies/mODEJHnPcfaZZnlohwufkM/WhatsApp-

appoints-grievance-officer-to-curb-fake-news-in-Ind.html.

77. Chakrabarti, Santanu, Lucile Stengel and Sapna Solanki, 'Duty, Identity, Credibility: Fake News and the Ordinary Citizen in India', accessed 26 July 2019, https://downloads.bbc.co.uk/mediacentre/duty-identity-credibility.pdf.

78. Mercier, Hugo and Dan Sperber, *The Enigma of Reason: a New Theory of Human Understanding*, Cambridge, MA: Harvard University Press, 2017.

79. Sloman, Steven A. and Philip Fernbach, *The Knowledge Illusion: Why We Never Think Alone*, New York: Riverhead Books, 2018.

80. Matthan, Rahul, 'The Backfire Effect and the Menace of Fake News', *Livemint*, 20 February 2018, https://www.livemint.com/Opinion/XdACMz4vMFqbYVyWoVb4VJ/The-backfire-effect-and-the-menace-of-fake-news.html.

81. Chakrabarti, Santanu, Lucile Stengel and Sapna Solanki, 'Duty, Identity, Credibility: Fake News and the Ordinary Citizen in India', accessed 26 July 2019, https://downloads.bbc.co.uk/mediacentre/duty-identity-credibility.pdf.

82. Desai, Nachiketa, 'Pratik Sinha of Alt News: Mischief Mongers Creating Havoc on Internet', *National Herald*, 28 April 2019, accessed 26 July 2019, https://www.nationalheraldindia.com/india/pratik-sinha-of-alt-news-mischief-mongers-creating-havoc-on-internet.

83. Doshi, Vidhi, 'India's Millions of New Internet Users Are Falling for Fake News—Sometimes with Deadly Consequences', *The Washington Post*, 1 October 2017, accessed 26 July 2019, https://www.washingtonpost.com/world/asia_pacific/indias-millions-of-new-internet-users-are-falling-for-fake-news--sometimes-with-deadly-consequences/2017/10/01/f078eaee-9f7f-11e7-8ed4-a750b67c552b_story.html?utm_term=.9d6618ff5d9c.

84. Shekhar, Divya, 'In a Post-truth World, "Check4Spam" Can Help You Sift Fake News', *The Economic Times*, 22 February 2017, accessed 26 July 2019, https://economictimes.indiatimes.com/magazines/panache/in-a-post-truth-world-check4spam-can-help-you-sift-fake-news/articleshow/57287228.cms?from=mdr.

85. Desai, Nachiketa, 'Pratik Sinha of Alt News: Mischief Mongers Creating Havoc on Internet', *National Herald*, 28 April 2019, accessed 26 July 2019,

https://www.nationalheraldindia.com/india/pratik-sinha-of-alt-news-mischief-mongers-creating-havoc-on-internet.

86. Pennycook, Gordon, Rand, David G., 'Who Falls for Fake News? The Roles of Bullshit Receptivity, Overclaiming, Familiarity, and Analytic Thinking', 22 March 2019.

87. Klapper, Joseph T., *The Effects of Mass Communication*: Glencoe: Free Press, 1960.

88. Cadwalladr, Carole., '"I Made Steve Bannon's Psychological Warfare Tool": Meet the Data War Whistleblower', *The Guardian*, 18 March 2018, accessed 26 July 2019, https://www.theguardian.com/news/2018/mar/17/data-war-whistleblower-christopher-wylie-faceook-nix-bannon-trump.

89. 'Suspending Cambridge Analytica and SCL Group from Facebook', Facebook Newsroom, accessed 26 July 2019, https://newsroom.fb.com/news/2018/03/suspending-cambridge-analytica/.

90. Harris, John, 'The Cambridge Analytica Saga Is a Scandal of Facebook's Own Making', *The Guardian*, 21 March 2018, accessed 26 July 2019, https://www.theguardian.com/commentisfree/2018/mar/21/cambridge-analytica-facebook-data-users-profit.

91. McNamee, Roger, *Zucked: Waking up to the Facebook Catastrophe*, New York: Penguin Press, 2019.

92. 'It's Not a Bug, It's a Feature: How Cambridge Analytica Demonstrates the Desperate Need for Data Protection', 21 March 2018, accessed 26 July 2019, https://www.accessnow.org/its-not-a-bug-its-a-feature-how-cambridge-analytica-demonstrates-the-desperate-need-for-data-protection/.

93. 'What We Know and What We Don't About What Cambridge Analytica Did in India', The Wire, accessed 26 July 2019, https://thewire.in/tech/what-we-know-and-what-we-dont-about-what-cambridge-analytica-did-in-india.

94. 'Govt Sends Second Set of Notices to Facebook, Cambridge Analytica', 25 April 2018, accessed 26 July 2019, https://www.thehindubusinessline.com/info-tech/govt-sends-second-set-of-notices-to-facebook-cambridge-analytica/article23673671.ece.

95. Vij, Shivam, 'The Inside Story of What Cambridge Analytica Actually

Did in India', ThePrint, 27 March 2018, accessed 26 July 2019, https://theprint.in/politics/exclusive-inside-story-cambridge-analytica-actually-india/44012/.
96. Ibid.
97. Punit, Itika Sharma, 'Cambridge Analytica's Parent Firm Proposed a Massive Political Machine for India's 2014 Elections', Quartz, 2 April 2018, accessed 26 July 2019, https://qz.com/1239561/cambridge-analyticas-parent-firm-proposed-a-massive-political-machine-for-indias-2014-elections/.
98. Vij, Shivam, 'Claims That Cambridge Analytica Did Political Work in India Are "absolutely False"', ThePrint, 29 March 2018, accessed 26 July 2019, https://theprint.in/politics/claims-that-cambridge-analytica-did-any-political-work-in-india-are-absolutely-false/45455/.
99. Gupta, Komal, 'Cambrige Analytica Whistleblower Christopher Wylie Tweets Details of India Operations', 28 March 2018, accessed 26 July 2019, https://www.livemint.com/Politics/CHlxMZEbw24tzCoirSGdGJ/Cambrige-Analytica-whistleblower-Christopher-Wylie-tweets-de.html.
100. 'Facebook Committed to Stopping Interference in Indian, U.S., Brazilian Elections: Zuckerberg', 22 March 2018, accessed 26 July 2019, https://www.thehindu.com/news/national/facebook-is-committed-to-stopping-interference-in-indian-elections-zuckerberg/article23318800.ece.
101. Wang, Yilun and Kosinski, Michal, 'Deep Neural Networks Are More Accurate than Humans at Detecting Sexual Orientation from Facial 10 Images', *Journal of Personality and Social Psychology* 114, no. 2 (February 2018): 246-57, doi:10.1037/pspa0000098.
102. Anderson, Drew, "Local Experts Call Report on Drinking During Pregnancy 'Flawed and Dangerous'", Glaad, 8 September 2017.
103. Murphy, Heather, 'Why Stanford Researchers Tried to Create a 'Gaydar' Machine', *The New York Times*, 9 October 2017, accessed 26 July 2019, https://www.nytimes.com/2017/10/09/science/stanford-sexual-orientation-study.html.
104. Kosinski, Michal, David Stillwell and Thore Graepel, 'Private Traits and Attributes Are Predictable from Digital Records of Human Behaviour', PNAS, 9 April 2013, accessed 26 July 2019, https://www.pnas.org/content/110/15/5802.

105. 'myPersonality project: Example of successful utilization of online social networks for large-scale social research', https://www.gsb.stanford.edu/sites/gsb/files/conf-presentations/stillwell_and_kosinski_2012.pdf
106. Lapowsky, Issie, 'The Man Who Saw the Dangers of Cambridge Analytica Years Ago', Wired, 19 June 2018, accessed 26 July 2019, https://www.wired.com/story/the-man-who-saw-the-dangers-of-cambridge-analytica/.
107. De Raad, B., *The Big Five Personality Factors: The Psycholexical Approach to Personality*, Ashland, OH, US: Hogrefe & Huber Publishers, 2000.
108. http://psych.colorado.edu/~carey/courses/psyc5112/readings/psnstructure_goldberg.pdf.
109. Cattell, R.B., 'The Description of Personality: Basic Traits Resolved into Clusters', *The Journal of Abnormal and Social Psychology*, 38(4), 476–506, 1943.
110. 'Personality Type Explained', HumanMetrics, accessed 26 July 2019, http://www.humanmetrics.com/personality/type.
111. Matz, S.C., M. Kosinski, G. Nave, and D.J. Stillwell, 'Psychological Targeting as an Effective Approach to Digital Mass Persuasion', PNAS, 28 November 2017, accessed 26 July 2019, https://www.pnas.org/content/114/48/12714/.
112. Sample, Ian, 'One Facebook 'Like' Is All It Takes to Target Adverts, Academics Find', *The Guardian*, 13 November 2017, accessed 26 July 2019, https://www.theguardian.com/science/2017/nov/13/facebook-likes-targeted-advertising-psychological-persuasion-academics-research.
113. Bodó, B. & Helberger, N. & de Vreese, C.H., 'Political Micro-targeting: A Manchurian Candidate or Just a Dark Horse?', *Internet Policy Review*, 6(4), 2017, DOI: 10.14763/2017.4.776
114. 'Congress Will Get 130 Seats Says Kamal Nath', Zee News Malayalam, 15 May 2019, accessed 26 July 2019, https://zeenews.india.com/malayalam/india/congress-will-get-130-seats-says-kamal-nath-27792.
115. Hersh, Eitan, *Hacking the Electorate: How Campaigns Perceive Voters*, New York: Cambridge University Press, 2015.
116. Ghosh, Snehashish, 'Electoral Databases—Privacy and Security Concerns', Centre for Internet & Society, 16 January 2014, accessed

26 July 2019, https://cis-india.org/internet-governance/blog/electoral-databases-2013-privacy-and-security-concerns.

117. Deshpande, Rajeev, 'Over 1 Crore Flocked to Give BJP a "missed call"', *The Times of India*, 12 May 2014, accessed 26 July 2019, https://timesofindia.indiatimes.com/news/Over-1-crore-flocked-to-give-BJP-a-missed-call/articleshow/34999013.cms.
118. Singh, Shivam Shankar, *How to Win an Indian Election: What Political Parties Don't Want You to Know*, Penguin Ebury Press, 2019.
119. Ullekh, NP, *War Room: The People, Tactics and Technology behind Narendra Modi's 2014 Win*, Roli Books, 2015.
120. Singh, Shivam Shankar, *How to Win an Indian Election: What Political Parties Don't Want You to Know*, Penguin Ebury Press, 2019.
121. Dasgupta, Piyasree, 'How to Spot a BJP Voter in Kolkata, Where No One's Saying "Jai Shri Ram" Aloud"', HuffPost India, 15 November 2018, accessed 26 July 2019, https://www.huffingtonpost.in/2018/11/14/elections-2019-how-the-bjp-in-bengal-is-shopping-for-voters-using-facebook-and-whatsapp_a_23589535/.
122. Trivedi, Ishita, 'Maneka Gandhi's Threat to Single out Muslim Voters Isn't a Bluff. India's Ballot Is No Longer Secret', Scroll.in, 16 April 2019, accessed 26 July 2019, https://scroll.in/article/920199/maneka-gandhis-threat-to-single-out-muslim-voters-isnt-a-bluff-indias-ballot-is-no-longer-secret.
123. Lasania, Yunus Y., 'YSRCP Alleges IT Grids Conspiring to Create Disturbances on Counting Day', 30 April 2019, accessed 26 July 2019, https://www.livemint.com/elections/lok-sabha-elections/ysrcp-alleges-it-grids-conspiring-to-create-disturbances-on-counting-day-1556627917542.html.
124. 'TDP App Under Probe For Profiling Voters on Caste, Party Leanings', The Quint, 1 March 2019, accessed 26 July 2019, https://www.thequint.com/news/india/elections-2019-seva-mitra-tdp-app-probe-voter-privacy-data-breach.
125. 'Narendra Modi App Has a Fake News Problem', HuffPost India, 27 January 2019, https://www.huffingtonpost.in/entry/narendra-modi-app-has-a-fake-news-problem_in_5c4d5c86e4b0287e5b8b6d52
126. Ibid.

127. Ibid.
128. Chaudhry, Apurva, 'BJP and the 'Silver Touch' of Trending Lies', NewsClick, 25 October 2017, accessed 26 July 2019, https://www.newsclick.in/bjp-and-silver-touch-trending-lies.
129. Abraham, Bobins, 'BJP Admits That It's Running NaMo TV On DTH Despite Ban By Election Commission', Indiatimes.com, 11 April 2019, accessed 26 July 2019, https://www.indiatimes.com/news/india/bjp-finally-owns-up-namo-tv-as-the-channel-continues-to-be-on-air-even-after-election-commission-order-365229.html.
130. Sebastian, Meryl, 'What on Earth Is Going on with NaMo TV?' HuffPost India, 4 April 2019, accessed 26 July 2019, https://www.huffingtonpost.in/entry/what-on-earth-is-going-on-with-namo-tv_in_5ca5b079e4b0409b0ec3a501.
131. https://shodhganga.inflibnet.ac.in/bitstream/10603/94199/7/07_chapter%202.pdf
132. Abraham, Bobins, 'BJP Admits That It's Running NaMo TV On DTH Despite Ban By Election Commission', Indiatimes.com, 11 April 2019, accessed 26 July 2019, https://www.indiatimes.com/news/india/bjp-finally-owns-up-namo-tv-as-the-channel-continues-to-be-on-air-even-after-election-commission-order-365229.html.
133. Memon, Zaheer, 'The Case That Shook India: Indira Gandhi vs Raj Narain', Courting The Law, 15 May 2019, accessed 26 July 2019, http://courtingthelaw.com/2019/05/15/laws-judgments-2/judgment-analysis/the-case-that-shook-india-indira-gandhi-vs-raj-narain/.
134. http://pib.nic.in/newsite/PrintRelease.aspx?relid=108926.
135. Staff, Scroll, 'Government Website Leaked 1.3 Lakh Aadhaar Numbers, Linked Them with Caste, Religion: Researcher', Scroll.in, 24 April 2018, accessed 26 July 2019, https://scroll.in/latest/876775/government-website-leaked-1-3-lakh-aadhaar-numbers-linked-them-with-caste-religion-researcher.
136. Lasania, Yunus Y., 'YSRCP Alleges IT Grids Conspiring to Create Disturbances on Counting Day', 30 April 2019, accessed 26 July 2019, https://www.livemint.com/elections/lok-sabha-elections/ysrcp-alleges-it-grids-conspiring-to-create-disturbances-on-counting-day-1556627917542.html.

137. Levitsky, Steven and Daniel Ziblatt, *How Democracies Die*, New York: Broadway Books, 2019.
138. Bermeo, Nancy, 'On Democratic Backsliding', *Journal of Democracy* 27, 1 (January 2016): 5–19, accessed 27 July 2019, https://www.journalofdemocracy.org/articles/on-democratic-backsliding/.
139. Tufekci, Zeynep, *Twitter and Tear Gas: The Power and Fragility of Networked Protest*, New Haven: Yale University Press, 2017.
140. Sinha, Amber, Questions of Fact: India's Aadhaar Matter and the Limits of the Supreme Court, (2018) IFRI, available at https://www.ifri.org/en/publications/notes-de-lifri/asie-visions/questions-fact-indias-aadhaar-matter-and-limits-supreme.
141. Nair, Remya, 'The Curious Case of Money Bills', 17 March 2016, accessed 26 July 2019, https://www.livemint.com/Politics/d8VEVxoVRFD4l4qBg6OQTP/The-curious-case-of-money-bills.html.
142. 'Lok Sabha Elections 2019: Key Statistics & Facts You Should Know', News18, 24 May 2019, accessed 26 July 2019, https://www.news18.com/photogallery/politics/lok-sabha-elections-2019-key-statistics-and-facts-you-should-to-know-2086101-9.html.
143. 'Election 2019: 2.7 Lakh Paramilitary, 20 Lakh State Police Personnel Deployed For Lok Sabha Polls', BloombergQuint, 28 April 2019, accessed 26 July 2019, https://www.bloombergquint.com/elections/election-2019-27-lakh-paramilitary-20-lakh-state-police-personnel-deployed-for-lok-sabha-polls.
144. Mehta, Pratap Bhanu, *The Burden of Democracy*, New Delhi: Penguin Books, 2003.
145. Ibid.
146. Shani, Ornit, *How India Became Democratic Citizenship and the Making of the Universal Franchise*, Cambridge: Cambridge University Press, 2018.
147. Shani, Ornit, 'Origins of Trust in India's Electoral Process' in Quraishi, S.Y. *The Great March of Democracy: Seven Decades of India's Elections*. Gurgaon: Vintage, an Imprint of Penguin Random House, 2019.
148. Shani, Ornit, 'Origins of Trust in India's Electoral Process' in Quraishi, S.Y. *The Great March of Democracy: Seven Decades of India's Elections*. Gurgaon: Vintage, an Imprint of Penguin Random House, 2019.
149. Jalan, Trisha, '30 Lakh Voters Deleted from AP and Telangana Electoral

Rolls: Report', MediaNama, 1 March 2019, accessed 26 July 2019, https://www.medianama.com/2019/03/223-aadhaar-33-lakh-voters-deleted-andhra-pradesh-telangana/.

150. Bhatia, Gautam, 'Opinion : The Election Commission Must Come Clean on the Deletion of Voters', *Hindustan Times*, 2 April 2019, accessed 26 July 2019, https://www.hindustantimes.com/analysis/the-election-commission-must-come-clean-on-the-deletion-of-voters/story-RpYyepCp2X4ibI4qYdDuhN.html.

151. Reddy, Sudhakar, 'Telangana Assembly Elections: Did Aadhar-EPIC Seeding Trigger Deletion of Voters?' *The Times of India*, 9 December 2018, Accessed 26 July 2019, https://timesofindia.indiatimes.com/city/hyderabad/telangana-assembly-elections-did-aadhar-epic-seeding-trigger-deletion-of-voters/article-show/67008173.cms.

152. 'Illegal Access to Data of Andhra Pradesh Voters: IT Firm Got Illegal Access to Data of Andhra Pradesh Voters: Telangana Police', *The Times of India*, 4 March 2019, accessed 26 July 2019, https://timesofindia.indiatimes.com/city/hyderabad/it-firm-got-illegal-access-to-data-of-andhra-pradesh-voters-telangana-police/articleshow/68260221.cms.

153. Sathe, Gopal, 'Hacking Democracy: How Stolen Aadhaar Data Of Nearly 10 Cr Voters Was Used To Delete People From Electoral Rolls', HuffPost India, 19 April 2019, accessed 26 July 2019, https://www.huffingtonpost.in/entry/hacking-democracy-stolen-aadhaar-voter-deletion_in_5cb9afa2e4b068d795cb870c.

154. Raman, Anuradha, 'Is Election Commission of India Toothless or Is It Refusing to Bite?' *The Hindu*, 19 April 2019, accessed 26 July 2019, https://www.thehindu.com/opinion/op-ed/is-the-election-commission-toothless-or-is-it-refusing-to-bite/article26878777.ece.

155. Anuja, 'Social Media Firms Come up with Ethics Code for Lok Sabha Polls', 20 March 2019, accessed 26 July 2019, https://www.livemint.com/elections/lok-sabha-elections/social-media-firms-come-up-with-ethics-code-for-lok-sabha-polls-1553101059336.html.

156. 'Verification for Election Advertising in India—Advertising Policies Help', Google, accessed 26 July 2019, https://support.google.com/adspolicy/answer/9224851?hl=en.

157. Singh, Nidhi and Chawla, Gunjan, 'Election Advertising on Social Media

Platforms: Is the Election Commission Outsourcing Regulation to the Private Sector?' Centre for Communication Governance, National Law University Delhi, 13 May 2019, accessed 26 July 2019, https://ccgdelhi.org/2019/05/02/election-advertising-on-social-media-platforms-is-the-election-commission-outsourcing-regulation-to-the-private-sector/.
158. https://www.lokniti.org/media/PDF-upload/1536927349_77426500_download_report.pdf.
159. Ullekh, NP, *War Room: The People, Tactics and Technology behind Narendra Modi's 2014 Win*, Roli Books, 2015.
160. Udupa, Sahana, 'India Needs a Fresh Strategy to Tackle Online Extreme Speech', Economic and Political Weekly, 11 February 2019, accessed 26 July 2019, https://www.epw.in/engage/article/election-2019-india-needs-fresh-strategy-to-tackle-new-digital-tools.
161. Pahwa, Nikhil, 'Govt of India Says Law of Abetment Applies to Social Media Platforms If They Do Not Act on Large Scale Misuse', MediaNama, 27 July 2018, accessed 26 July 2019, https://www.medianama.com/2018/07/223-govt-law-abetment-social-media-fake-news/.
162. Reddy, Prashant, 'Cambridge Analytica and Facebook—Is Anybody Actually Liable Under Indian Law?' The Wire, 3 April 2018, accessed 26 July 2019, https://thewire.in/law/cambridge-analytica-facebook-liability-indian-law.
163. Press Trust of India, 'IT Ministry Mulls Third Notice to WhatsApp; May Insist on Message Trail', *Business Standard*, 20 September 2018, accessed 26 July 2019, https://www.business-standard.com/article/current-affairs/govt-mulls-third-notice-to-whatsapp-may-insist-on-message-traceability-118092000692_1.html.
164. Kumaraguru, Ponnurangam, 'Twitter's "suspect Users" Affects Indian Political Handles, 8 February 2019, accessed 26 July 2019, http://precog.iiitd.edu.in/blog/2019/02/08/twitters-suspect-users-affects-indian-political-handles/.
165. 'Twitter Cracks down on Fake Accounts; PM Modi, Rahul Gandhi Find Themselves Lot Less Popular', *Business Today*, 11 February 2019, accessed 26 July 2019, https://www.businesstoday.in/current/economy-politics/twitter-cracks-down-on-fake-accounts-pm-modi-rahul-gandhi-find-

themselves-lot-less-popular/story/318467.html.
166. 'The Bazee.com Saga Unravelled: Supreme Court Clarifies Intermediary Liabilities for Hosting Obscene Content', Nishith Desai Associates, 15 February 2017, accessed 26 July 2019, http://www.nishithdesai.com/information/news-storage/news-details/article/the-bazeecom-saga-unravelled-supreme-court-clarifies-intermediary-liabilities-for-hosting-obscene.html.
167. Dara, Rishabh, 'Intermediary Liability in India: Chilling Effects on Free Expression on the Internet', Centre for Internet & Society, 27 April 2012, accessed 26 July 2019, https://cis-india.org/internet-governance/chilling-effects-on-free-expression-on-internet.
168. Shrivastava, Prachi, 'Behind the Scenes: How 90 Lawyers & 3 Judges Created the Biggest Free Speech Judgment in More than Half a Century', Legally India—News for Lawyers, 1 April 2015, accessed 26 July 2019, https://www.legallyindia.com/the-bench-and-the-bar/behind-the-scenes-how-90-lawyers-3-judges-created-the-biggest-free-speech-judgment-in-more-than-half-a-century-20150401-5767.
169. Bakshy, Eytan, Lada Adamic and Solomon Messing, 'Exposure to Diverse Information on Facebook', Facebook Research, 14 January 2017, accessed 26 July 2019, https://research.fb.com/blog/2015/05/exposure-to-diverse-information-on-facebook-2/.
170. Kirkpatrick, David, 'The Facebook Defect: How Mark Zuckerberg Disregarded Privacy', *Time*, 12 April 2018, accessed 26 July 2019, https://time.com/5237458/the-facebook-defect/.
171. Jonnalagadda, Harish, 'YouTube Has Over 245 Million Monthly Active Users in India', Android Central, 28 August 2018, accessed 26 July 2019, https://www.androidcentral.com/youtube-has-245-million-monthly-active-users-india.
172. Sunstein, Cass R., *Republic: Divided Democracy in the Age of Social Media*, Princeton: Princeton University Press, 2017.
173. Miere, Jason Le, 'Trump's Tweets Are "Official Statements", Says Sean Spicer, Completely Contradicting White House Aides', Newsweek, 6 June 2017, accessed 26 July 2019, https://www.newsweek.com/trump-tweets-spicer-official-statements-621919.
174. Global Freedom of Expression, Columbia University, https://

globalfreedomofexpression.columbia.edu/cases/knight-first-amendment-institute-v-donald-j-trump/.

175. Gupta, Apar, 'Unconstitutional Twitter Blocks', Medium, 12 August 2017, accessed 26 July 2019, https://apargupta.com/unconstitutional-twitter-blocks-6d0549d90c09.

176. Jawed, Sam, 'UIDAI Denies Blocking Anyone from Their Official Twitter Accounts in an RTI Response, Twitter Users Call It a Bluff', AltNews, 30 April 2017, accessed 26 July 2019, https://www.altnews.in/uidai-denies-blocking-anyone-official-twitter-accounts-rti-response-twitter-users-call-bluff/.

177. Tufekci, Zeynep, *Twitter and Tear Gas: The Power and Fragility of Networked Protest*, New Haven: Yale University Press, 2017.

178. Varadarajan, Siddharth, 'Times Now First Denies Airing Doctored Video, Then Concedes It Did', The Wire, 20 February 2016, accessed 26 July 2019, https://thewire.in/media/times-nows-first-denies-airing-doctored-video-then-concedes-it-did.

179. Files, John, 'Lee Loevinger, 91, Kennedy-Era Antitrust Chief', *The New York Times*, 8 May 2004, accessed 26 July 2019, https://www.nytimes.com/2004/05/08/us/lee-loevinger-91-kennedy-era-antitrust-chief.html.

180. Bork, Robert H., *The Antitrust Paradox*, New York: Free Press, 1964.

181. Bork, Robert H., 'Legislative Intent and the Policy of the Sherman Act', *Journal of Law and Economics* 9, 7 (1966) 45-47.

182. Odrozek, Kasia, 'More than 90% of the World Uses Google Search', Mozilla, 4 May 2018, accessed 26 July 2019, https://internethealthreport.org/2018/90-of-the-world-uses-google-search/.

183. Ip, Greg, 'The Antitrust Case against Facebook, Google and Amazon', The Wall Street Journal, 16 January 2018, accessed 26 July 2019, https://www.wsj.com/articles/the-antitrust-case-against-facebook-google-amazon-and-apple-1516121561?mod=e2fb&fbclid=IwAR2-BlQ_kuQynGEmI49U450cXmWWvHhfjhw-iy5odR0bUSxoG1ZuNj266es.

184. Baublitz, Joseph, 'M&A Explained: The Amazon—Whole Foods Merger', *Juris Magazine*, 14 April 2018, accessed 26 July 2019, http://sites.law.duq.edu/juris/2018/01/12/ma-explained-the-amazon-whole-foods-merger/.

185. Dans, Enrique, 'Amazon Takes Vertical Integration to a New Level', Medium, 10 February 2018, accessed 26 July 2019, https://medium.com/enrique-dans/amazon-takes-vertical-integration-to-a-new-level-d9fd65d4d06d.
186. Krazit, Tom, 'Google to Stop Censoring in China, May Pull out', CNET, 12 January 2010, accessed 26 July 2019, https://www.cnet.com/news/google-to-stop-censoring-in-china-may-pull-out/.
187. Levin, Dan, 'China Escalating Attack on Google', *The New York Times*, 2 June 2014, accessed 26 July 2019, https://www.nytimes.com/2014/06/03/business/chinas-battle-against-google-heats-up.html.
188. Conger, Kate and Daisuke Wakabayashi, 'Google Employees Protest Secret Work on Censored Search Engine for China', *The New York Times*, 16 August 2018, accessed 26 July 2019, https://www.nytimes.com/2018/08/16/technology/google-employees-protest-search-censored-china.html.
189. Dhara, Tushar, 'Why Did Facebook Stop the Promotion of The Caravan's Story on Amit Shah and Jay Shah?' *The Caravan*, 13 October 2018, accessed 26 July 2019, https://caravanmagazine.in/media/why-did-facebook-stop-the-promotion-of-the-caravans-story-on-amit-shah-and-jay-shah.
190. Jalan, Trisha, 'Facebook Blocks Accounts of a Dozen Indian Journalists: Report', MediaNama, 8 October 2018, accessed 26 July 2019, https://www.medianama.com/2018/10/223-facebook-blocks-indian-journalists-report/.
191. Jalan, Trisha, 'Facebook: 5 New Fact-checkers for India, Regulation in Germany, Canada and Startup Acquisition', MediaNama, 12 February 2019, accessed 26 July 2019, https://www.medianama.com/2019/02/223-facebook-digest/.
192. Bhat, Prajwal, 'Fighting Fake News: Inside Karnataka's Virtual Campaign Trail', The News Minute, 10 May 2018, accessed 26 July 2019, https://www.thenewsminute.com/article/fighting-fake-news-inside-karnatakas-virtual-campaign-trail-81042.
193. PTI, 'Facebook Removes Nearly 700 Pages Linked to Congress Due to 'inauthentic Behaviour', *The Economic Times*, 1 April 2019, accessed 26 July 2019, https://economictimes.indiatimes.com/news/elections/lok-

sabha/india/facebook-removes-687-pages-linked-to-congress-party-due-to-coordinated-inauthentic-behaviour/articleshow/68669174.cms.
194. PTI, 'Ground Zero: Logging into Facebook's Election War Room', 8 April 2019, accessed 26 July 2019, https://www.thehindubusinessline.com/info-tech/social-media/ground-zero-logging-into-facebooks-election-war-room/article26771487.ece.
195. Sathe, Gopal, 'How the BJP Automated Political Propaganda on WhatsApp', HuffPost India, 19 April 2019, accessed 26 July 2019, https://www.huffingtonpost.in/entry/bjp-automated-political-propaganda-whatsapp-sarv_in_5cb62076e4b082aab08d7f18.
196. IANS, 'WhatsApp Tipline of No Use for 2019 Lok Sabha Polls', *The Economic Times*, 6 April 2019, accessed 26 July 2019, https://economictimes.indiatimes.com/tech/software/whatsapp-tipline-of-no-use-for-2019-lok-sabha-polls/articleshow/68734867.cms.
197. PTI, 'BJP Declares Rs 1,027-crore Income in FY18: Report', *The Economic Times*, 17 December 2018, accessed 26 July 2019, https://m.economictimes.com/news/politics-and-nation/bjp-declares-rs-1027-crore-income-in-fy18-report/articleshow/67133806.cms.
198. Twitter Safety, 'Strengthening Our Approach to Deliberate Attempts to Mislead Voters', 24 April 2019, https://blog.twitter.com/en_us/topics/company/2019/strengthening-our-approach-to-deliberate-attempts-to-mislead-vot.html
199. Vishnoi, Anubhuti, 'Electoral Bonds: Ruling BJP Bags 95% of Funds', *The Economic Times*, 29 November 2018, accessed 26 July 2019, https://economictimes.indiatimes.com/news/politics-and-nation/electoral-bonds-ruling-bjp-bags-95-of-funds/articleshow/66858037.cms?from=mdr.
200. Ramani, Srinivasan, 'Electoral bonds benefited BJP the most, cut cash component of donations', *The Economic Times*, 29 November 2018, accessed 17 August 2019, https://www.thehindu.com/news/national/poll-bonds-benefited-bjp-the-most-cut-cash-component-of-donations/article26891622.ece

Made in the USA
Monee, IL
03 May 2026